BETWEEN THE GOD OF THE PROPHETS AND THE GOD OF THE PHILOSOPHERS

Reflections of an Athari on the Divine Attributes

Hatem al-Haj

Edited by
Jamila Hakam

BETWEEN THE GOD OF THE PROPHETS AND THE GOD OF THE PHILOSOPHERS

Cover designed by Janis Mahnure and Moataz Ahmed

Visit my website at www.drhatemalhaj.com

Printed in the United States of America

First Printing: March 9, 2020

ISBN-13: 979-8-6161813-3-6

Contents

بسم الله

والحمد لله

والصلاة والسلام على رسول الله

INTRODUCTION

Peter Westh, a lecturer in the History of Religions,[1] said, "That anthropomorphism is indeed a universal trait of religions the world over has been acknowledged by generations of scholars of religion."[2] The charge of anthropomorphism is not a new one, and it is not directed solely against one group of religionists. The concept of a "personal" God is expected to be utterly rejected by atheists. But they are not alone. It is very possible that agnosticism and negative theology will take the place of absolute atheism, not necessarily in compliance with the Hegelian trajectory of historical *dialektik*,[3] but because atheism has some major difficulties. At the intellectual level, it is hard to convince people that this existence has no maker or cause, and, at both intellectual and emotional

---

[1] A lecturer in the History of Religions at the Department of Cross-Cultural and Regional Studies, University of Copenhagen, Denmark.

[2] Westh, Peter. "Anthropomorphism in God Concepts: The Role of Narrative," In *Origins of Religion, Cognition and Culture*, ed. Armin Geertz (Abingdon, UK: Routledge, 2007), 396–414.

[3] Which claims that history does not move in linear lines, but along a trajectory of thesis–antithesis–synthesis, although Hegel himself did not use these exact words.

levels, it is hard to convince them that it has no purpose or meaning. Since the 1970s, we have witnessed an increased interest in the concept of *apophasis* in the study of religion, which is described as a "new, ethicalized divine transcendence."[4] The apophatic god of negative theology will provide some explanation and comfort without intervening in our lives. After all, nothing can be demanded by a god of which nothing can be predicated and about which nothing can be said. It is a forever silenced god. It is the areligious philosophers' preferred god (at least from the time of Aristotle); a god which is remote, detached, and can hardly be an object of adoration or worship, even though it may be an object of wonderment.

When AMJA was planning its 17th Annual Imams' Conference about atheism, I was asked to contribute with a paper. I thought it would be befitting to address the depiction of a "personal" God in the theistic traditions, and the contesting depictions. Being an Athari (scripturalist) in my creedal orientation, I felt this to be even more binding on me. However, there is a growing sense of aversion to and exhaustion from intra-Islamic polemics on creed, and a detailed discussion of the topic of the Divine attributes can never steer clear of controversy. It is my belief, though, that an avoidance of such detailed discussions is

---

[4] Aydogan Kars, "Unsaying God: Negative Theology in Medieval Islam" (New York: Oxford University Press, 2019; Oxford Scholarship Online, 2019), https://doi.org/10.1093/oso/9780190942458.001.0001.

unwarranted and dangerous. A void that might be left by the different Muslim groups will be filled by non-Muslim philosophies and belief systems. "Polemics" have been a part of the Islamic discourse since the time of the Companions. In fact, it would not be far-fetched to say that disagreement helped define the borders of "orthodoxy" as much as agreement did. With the lack of a papacy or Divine communication to anyone after the Seal of the Messengers (pbuh), it was the multilateral and transgenerational discourse among Muslim scholars that delineated the borders of "orthodox" understanding of the Revelation. How do we then proceed with a necessary polemical discourse while mitigating most of its untoward side effects? Well, a long answer would require a separate paper on *adâb al-ikhtilâf* (etiquettes of disagreement), but the short and most pertinent answer here, I believe, lies in two proposals.

1- Measured exposure

This is not a generic prescription to water down the discourse on creed for all audiences. However, for the public, I would support a basic explanation of the tenets of *'aqeedah* from a book like *al-Ṭaḥâwiyyah* or the introduction of *al-Risâlah* by Ibn Abi Zayd al-Qayrawâni (rA). After erecting enough guardrails, there should be an emphasis on the generation, strengthening, and refinement of faith, which is something the conventional *'aqeedah* discourse of various schools does not provide:

but the *tazkiyyah/taṣawwuf* discourse does. While this is my general advice for teaching beginners, it would not be enough for the advanced students and those who would be entrusted with clarifying or even defending the intricacies of Islamic creed. It is also not enough for many of our youth, who have significant exposure to philosophical discourses on metaphysics or other theistic belief systems. Finally, we must also account for the effect of the cultural themes that surround us, continually embedding subliminal messages in our subconsciousness. These influences continue to remold our perspective and tarnish our *fiṭrah* (original disposition), and without proper rehabilitation of it, the Islamic discourse on divinities and many other concepts will sound odder and odder.

2- Disagree and Love

It is true that one may develop a special affinity toward the teachers with greatest impact on them, so it may be natural for a Ḥanbali to have a special place for Imam Ahmad in their heart. However, this should not mean less *walâ'* (religious allegiance and love) for Imam Abu Ḥanifah, for instance. The same for a student with a Ghazalian or Taymiyyan orientation: their greater intellectual indebtedness to one of them should not translate into less *walâ'* or respect for the person of the other. It should also not mean approval of one teacher's entire legacy or rejection or neglect of another's. Partisanship and compartmentalization can have detrimental effects on our intellectual integrity and vigor, as well as on our spiritual wellness.

We can focus on the issues while safeguarding our *walâ'* for all bearers of the tradition who meant well for this *deen* and for this *Ummah*. The Quran reminds us often of our human brotherhood, and if we were loyal to its legacy, we must love all our brethren. Those among them who are Muslim deserve another type of love, forged in our spiritual brotherhood. I would not limit this to the different strands considered generally of Ahl al-Sunnah wa al-Jamâ'ah,[5] but I would argue here that those of the Mu'tazilah, for instance, who meant to serve Allah and His *deen*, deserve their share of this love as well. Many of them led exemplary lives and made great contributions to Islam's cause. If we do not find room in our hearts for them, our love reserves must be exceptionally depleted.

Even when we focus on the issues, we should avoid exaggerating the danger of the opposite position, because it is often used as a pretext to justify the demonization of the opponents. You will see later in this work the transgenerational discourse between luminaries like Ibn Rushd, al-Râzi, and Ibn Taymiyyah (may Allah have mercy

---

[5] 'People of the Sunnah and the Community'; also called "Ahl al-Sunnah" for short.

on them all). That discourse was on the presumption of conflict between reason and Revelation. While this Athari writer will adopt Ibn Taymiyyah's position, he recognizes the indebtedness of his thesis (or synthesis) to those of his predecessors, including people who were his diametrical opponents, like Ibn Sina (Avicenna).[6]-[i] I also recognize how, within their intellectual paradigms, each one of them meant to preserve the integrity of the Revelation without impugning the office of reason.

---

[6] While Ibn Sina (rA) was declared an unbeliever by several imams like al-Ghazâli, Ibn Taymiyyah and others because of some major heresies, including his belief in the "beginningless" eternity of the world and his rejection of the resurrection of bodies, it was reported that he repented and would recite the whole Quran every three days prior to his death. Some jurists may have certainty about the disbelief of a person because of what they have come to know about them. This certainty varies among different individuals because of what they have known in support of hereticating them and against it: hence, the disagreements over such declarations. Hereticating Muslims is always a perilous undertaking, and when in doubt, we must refrain from it. The fact that Ibn Sina had this commitment to the Book of Allah at the end of his life is sufficient *mâni'* (hindrance) to refrain personally from excommunicating him. It is possible that his "intellectual intoxication" led him to those heresies, so we declare our disavowal of them, and we ask for his forgiveness. Finally, as Imam al-Dhahabi said, "He who was declared an unbeliever because of a heresy, regardless of its magnitude, is not like the original unbelievers or the Jews and Zoroastrians. Those who believed in Allah, His Messenger, and the hereafter, and fasted, prayed, made hajj, and paid zakat, Allah refuses to hold them equal to those who opposed the Messenger, worshiped idols, and denounced the laws and rejected the religion, even if the first committed enormities, went astray, and innovated (in the deen). Yet, we declare to Allah our disavowal of innovation and its people" (See Shams al-Deen Muhammad ibn Ahmad al-Dhahabi, *Siyar A'lâm al-Nubalâ'* [Cairo: Dâr al-Ḥadeeth, 1427/2006], 8:337).

As an Athari, I do recognize (and regret) how some people, largely of my creedal orientation, have contributed lately to inflaming the intra-Islamic debate on matters of creed and others. I do, however, recognize that the hardcore of all groups share the same belligerence toward their opponents. In fact, you will rarely (if ever) find the same level of hatred and hostility some people of the Ash'ari persuasion have for Imam Ibn Taymiyyah exhibited by any Atharis toward Imam al-Ghazâli, for instance. And while many Ash'aris are so adamant on circulating the dispraise of Imam Ibn Taymiyyah by other scholars, you will rarely find Atharis as adamantly circulating the equally extreme dispraise of Imam al-Ghazâli by the likes of Imams al-Ṭarṭooshi, al-Mâziri, 'Iyâḍ, Ibn al-Jawzi, and others, which for some reached the level of contingent excommunication and caused some to issue legal verdicts in favor of burning his books. Also, historically, Atharis have frequently been the object of this hostility. You find *takfeer* (excommunication)[7] and *la'n* (invocation of curses) too often in the writings of many theologians, both scripturalists and rationalists, to the point that al-'Izz ibn 'Abd al-Salam (rA), who is largely in agreement with the Ash'aris, marveled at their frequent *takfeer* (excommunication) of their opponents in his book

[7] *Takfeer* is a verbal noun that means declaring someone a disbeliever (*kâfir*). While excommunication was first used within a Christian context, it is a suitable translation of *takfeer*.

Qawâ ʿid al-Aḥkâm.[8-ii] Allah knows that I do not say this out of partisanship or in defense of my "group," because being cured from groupism is what I wish for myself and my fellow Muslims, but reconciliation and acceptance starts from within and with self-acceptance—of course without self-delusion. Whatever excuses they may have had, and the different circumstances and paradigms they operated from, we must think good of them, but it is my hope that we reach a "common word" on a conciliatory trajectory from here that would protect the unity of the Ummah, preserve the integrity of the tradition, and save the honor of its bearers.

Finally, Atharis (scripturalists) did not seek to undermine the office of reason, nor did *Mutakallimoon* (rationalist theologians) seek to undermine the epistemic value of the scriptures. Rather, one group saw intractable conflicts between reason and some *ẓawâhir* (primary meanings) of the scriptural reports, whereas the other did not acknowledge the presence of conflict. While there may be clear leanings justifying these labels, the division is not absolute, and as we may see in the typology of positions and the following discussions, there is no uniformity within any of the referenced groups. It is my hope that this work will help its English-speaking readers understand

---

8 'Izz al-Deen Ibn 'Abd al-Salâm, *Qawâ ʿid al-Aḥkâm*, ed. Ṭâha 'Abd al-Ra'oof Sa'd (Cairo: Maktabat al-Kulliyât al-Azhariyyah, n.d.), 1:203.

the Islamic discourse concerning the Divine attributes and be able to construct a systematic argument in defense of the Islamic conception of God.

WHERE DO WE GET OUR BELIEF FROM? OUR EPISTEMOLOGICAL POSITION

□وَلِلَّهِ غَيْبُ السَّمَاوَاتِ وَالْأَرْضِ ۚ وَمَا أَمْرُ السَّاعَةِ
إِلَّا كَلَمْحِ الْبَصَرِ أَوْ هُوَ أَقْرَبُ ۚ إِنَّ اللَّهَ عَلَىٰ كُلِّ
شَيْءٍ قَدِيرٌ □ وَاللَّهُ أَخْرَجَكُم مِّن بُطُونِ أُمَّهَاتِكُمْ لَا
تَعْلَمُونَ شَيْئًا وَجَعَلَ لَكُمُ السَّمْعَ وَالْأَبْصَارَ
وَالْأَفْئِدَةَ ۙ لَعَلَّكُمْ تَشْكُرُونَ □

"And to Allah belongs the unseen [aspects] of the heavens and the earth. And the command for the Hour is not but as a glance of the eye or even nearer. Indeed, Allah is over all things competent. And Allah has extracted you from the wombs of your mothers not knowing a thing, and He made for you hearing and vision and intellect that perhaps you would be grateful." [Al-Naḥl 16:77-78][9]

---

[9] Unless otherwise mentioned, the English translation of the meanings of

This verse provides the outline of the Islamic theory of epistemology. It mentions three sources of knowledge in this order:

1. truthful reports (hearing)
2. empirical findings (sights)
3. reason (intellect/innate potency)

These are the sources of knowledge in general. But what about the knowledge of the *ghayb* (unseen)? It seems that empirical findings of the external senses have no place here. However, do we only perceive things with our external senses? Muslim scholars have argued that there is an internal sense (*ḥiss bâṭin*) with which we perceive real extant feelings of fear, sadness, joy, and so on.[10]-[iii] Muslim scholars contend that we perceive God, as well as our very souls, by our internal sense. Beyond that, we are left with truthful reports and reason. How does each of them contribute to our knowledge of the *ghayb*, particularly the Divine Himself, and what happens if what they contribute appear to conflict?

---

the Quran used throughout this paper is that of Sahih International, as found on Quran.com.

[10] Ibn Taymiyyah, Taqi al-Deen Ahmad ibn 'Abd al-Ḥaleem, *Dar' Ta'âruḍ al-'Aql wa al-Naql*, 2nd ed., ed. Muhammad Rashâd Sâlim (Riyadh: Mohammad Ibn Saud Islamic University, 1411/1991), 6:108.

The Role of Truthful Reports

﴿وَتَمَّتْ كَلِمَتُ رَبِّكَ صِدْقًا وَعَدْلًا ۚ لَا مُبَدِّلَ
لِكَلِمَاتِهِ ۚ وَهُوَ السَّمِيعُ الْعَلِيمُ﴾

> "And the word of your Lord has been fulfilled in truth and in justice. None can alter His words, and He is the Hearing, the Knowing."
> [Al-'An`âm 6:115]

The Revelation has been perfected in truth (concerning its declarative part) and in justice (concerning its imperative part).

If there is no way for our empirical experiences to apprehend God and no way for the internal sense or intellect to apprehend more than His existence and the perfection of His essential attributes, then we must be dependent on the Revelation for all other knowledge of Him and of the *ghayb*. The truth of the Revelation is established through the proofs of prophethood, so when one commits to unquestioning acceptance of its dicta, they are not being irrational or accepting faith blindly. Limiting knowledge to that which can be established through demonstrative proofs or empirical findings is an enormous error.

In the preface to the second edition of his *Critique of Pure Reason*, Kant says, "I have therefore found it necessary to deny knowledge, in order to make room for faith."[11] Though never a skeptic (for example, he was always committed to scientific knowledge), Kant came to limit knowledge to objects of possible experience, and to regard ideas of metaphysics (including theology) as matters of rational faith. We agree with Kant on the rationality of faith and on metaphysics being largely undiscoverable through empirical or rational investigation, but we disagree with him on limiting knowledge to those routes. After all, the people who saw Moses (pbuh) split the red sea, Jesus (pbuh) bring life to the dead, or an army drink from Muhammad's (pbuh) hand, should have more certainty regarding what these messengers had told them about the unseen than much of their own empirical findings. Most people had a justifiable certainty in the presence of China through concurrent reports of its existence. In the first case, the truthfulness of the reports was established through miracles and other definitive proofs, and in the second, it was established through concurrence of people with the impossibility of collusion. Demanding a higher level of certainty to be confident in the truth of what we know would lead to radical skepticism or even solipsism.

Having established that truthful reports are a valid source of knowledge, we must be aware that there are two factors to be considered here: the authenticity of transmission and the implications of such reports. As for

---

[11] Immanuel Kant, *Critique of Pure Reason*, trans. & ed. Paul Guyer and Allen W. Wood (Cambridge, 1999).

the implications, the importance of reason, linguistic conventions, contextuality, and intertextuality in our understanding of these reports will be discussed later. As for the transmission, there is no doubt about the transmission of the Quran and the *mutawâtir* Sunnah (conveyed through recurrent mass transmission). Other authentic reports with less certain transmission are still acceptable as a basis of practice according to all Sunni Muslims, and as a basis for secondary matters of creed[12-iv] as well, according to Atharis, whether or not they confer certainty. In fact, Imam Ibn 'Abd al-Barr (rA) considered the acceptance of singular reports in creedal issues a matter of agreement among Ahl al-Sunnah.[13-v]

---

[12] The foundations of creed, like the six pillars of faith, may not be established by speculative proofs, whether that uncertainty is in their transmission or implication. In *al-Musawwadah*, Ibn Taymiyyah relays from the imams of the Ḥanbali madhhab that in these matters, only singular reports that have been accepted by the Ummah are authoritative (See Ibn Taymiyyah, *Al-Musawwadah*, ed. Muhamamd Muḥyi al-Deen 'Abd al-Ḥameed [Beirut: Dâr al-Kitâb al-'Arabi, n.d.], 248). Ibn 'Abd al-Barr does not make that distinction when he accepts those reports in matters of creed. See the following footnote.

[13] Abu 'Umar Yoosuf ibn 'Abd Allâh al-Namari Ibn 'Abd al-Barr, *Al-Tamheed lima fil-Muwa▯▯â' min al-Ma'âni wal-Asâneed*, eds. Muṣṭafâ ibn Ahmad al-'Alawi and Muhammad 'Abd al-Kabeer al-Bakri (Morocco: Ministry of Endowments and Islamic Affairs, 1967), 1:8. There, he argues that they must be accepted in creedal matters, even though he recognizes that they do not confer certainty. Sometimes Atharis affirm that singular reports are used as a basis of creed (*'aqeedah*), but they would still say that they do not induce "*'ilm*," and by that they mean "certainty." Note that there is a disagreement about the certainty of some singular reports as those reported by both al-Bukhari and Muslim. The majority of

It is important to stress that weak reports must never be used as a basis for creed. At times, some Atharis erred in citing weak reports that have repugnant meanings. For example, Imam Abu Ya'la (rA) related a weak hadith from Jâbir ibn 'Abd Allâh:

> I heard the Messenger of God saying, "On the Day of Resurrection my community will arrive at a hill, placed above all the other nations. Each nation in its turn will be given its idols. Then our Lord will come to us by foot, and say [to the believers]: 'What are you waiting for?' And they will say: 'We are waiting for our Lord.' He shall respond: 'I am your Lord.' They will say: 'If only we could see you!' And then He shall be revealed to them laughing to such an extent that His uvulae [in another report: and molars] are seen. After that, they will start following Him."[14]

Abu Ya'lâ (rA) felt the unease in the report, so he explained:

> We do not assert [that God has] a laughter which includes the opening of the mouth, and grinning while showing the teeth. We do not assert [that God

---

scholars of *uṣool* still considered their transmission speculative.

[14] Abu Ya'la, *Ibṭâl al-Ta'weelât,* 214. Translation from Livnat Holtzman, " 'Does God Really Laugh?' – Appropriate and Inappropriate Descriptions of God in Islamic Traditionalist Theology," *Laughter in the Middle Ages and Early Modern Times* (*Fundamentals of Medieval and Early Modern Culture,* Vol. 5), 2010, Ch. 2., 165-200, https://doi.org/10.1515/9783110245486.165.

> has] molars and uvula, which are body organs and parts. What we assert is an attribute, even though we do not grasp its meaning. It is precisely the same as we assert [that God has] face and hands; that He hears and sees.[15]-[vi]

Before putting out an argument in defense of a creedal position, we must first ascertain its establishment. Imam Abu Ya'la (rA) did not need to defend a hadith that is not established in the first place.

The Role of Reason

We can imagine the role of reason in relation to the Revelation in one of three respects:

1. reason as a tool of understanding the Revelation
2. reason as an independent source of knowledge
3. reason in opposition to the apparent meanings of the Revelation

Reason as an independent source of metaphysical knowledge

The debate between the Continental Rationalists and British Empiricists culminated in the Kantian attempt at reconciliation between them by denying the Empiricists' notion that the mind is a blank slate waiting to be filled by empirical findings while also rejecting the Rationalists' notion that pure, *a priori* knowledge independent of the world exists. Reason is a potency that is constructed

---

[15] Abu Ya'la, *Ibṭâl al-Ta'weelât,* 218.Translation from Holtzman, "Does God Really Laugh?", pp. 165-200.

through our experience of the world, and the categories of our understanding (the duality of substance and accident, for instance) cannot be separated from our experiences of the world. Kant, therefore, did not believe that reason has much to say about metaphysical realities. Debates on rational metaphysics have been raging since the time of Plato. They were transmitted to our religious discourse: in particular, Aristotelian and Neoplatonic philosophy. The question Kant, arguably the most important philosopher in modern times, asked, is not whether a particular group was right, but whether rational metaphysics is at all rational!

Ibn Taymiyyah (rA) reported from Ahmad ibn Ḥanbal (rA) and al-Hârith al-Muḥâsibi (rA) that reason is a *ghareezah* (instinct), and from others that it is a *quwwah* (potency). He argued that reason helps to universalize particulars, issue judgments in the form of predicative statements (*tasdeeqât/aḥkâm*) relative to existent particulars, and draw inferences.[16]

This potency requires data so as to form judgments about particular existents. How can it then (independent of Revelation) issue predicative statements about the unseen? As we said before, it will have a limited, but still

---

[16] Carl Sharif El-Tobgui, *Reason, Revelation & the Reconstitution of Rationality: Taqī Al-Dīn Ibn Taymiyya's (d. 728/1328)* "Dar' Ta'ārud Al-Aql Wa-l-Naql" *or "The Refutation of the Contradiction of Reason and Revelation"* (Montreal: McGill University Libraries, 2013), 271.

vital, scope of operation there. It can realize the existence of God and the perfection of His essential attributes. However, its universalizing function will not help because of the great dissimilarity between the world of the *shahâdah* (seen) and that of the *ghayb* (unseen). What about rational inferences? Can they lead to knowledge? Of course, they may even lead to compelling (*ḍaroori*) knowledge, but only if the process of deduction is valid and the premises are irresistible. What can we then infer from *shahâdah* about *ghayb*? Nothing, really, except the existence of the Creator or "First Cause." Otherwise, there is nothing that is shared by them except the outward meanings of the names used by the Revelation and their being subject to the logical maxims such as the law of non-contradiction.[17] It is because of all this, and because of what many speculative theologians called *takâfu' al-adillah* (equivalency of proofs), that some of the most erudite among them realized the futility of reason as a source of metaphysical knowledge, which is attributed to many of the greatest *Mutakallimeen* (rationalist theologians), such as al-Muḥâsibi, al-Juwayni, al-Ghazâli, and al-Râzi (may Allah bestow mercy on them all). We read in the introduction to *Nihâyat al-Iqdâm fi 'ilm al-*

---

[17] Ibn Taymiyyah uses this often. Al-Juwayni uses it as well. For example, in *al-Irshâd* he uses it to tell the Bâṭiniyyah there is no middle ground between negation and affirmation. See Abu al-Ma'âli 'Abd al-Malik al-Juwayni, *al-Irshâd* (Cairo: Maktabat al-Thaqâfah al-Deeniyyah, 2015), 42.

Kalâm by al-Shahrastâni (rA) two verses highlighting the futility of speculative theology:

> I have made the rounds of the gatherings of the learned (*ma'âhid*)
> And cast my eyes upon the haunts of erudition (*ma'âlim*);
> Yet never did I see but men perplexed, with their chins in their hands
> Or gnashing their teeth in regret.[18]-[vii]

But is there still a place for rational inquiry in the discipline of creed?

The Place of *Kalâm*: Reason as a Tool of Understanding and Armor for Defense

Should reason really be excluded from any discourse on creed in favor of the letter of Revelation? Why? Shouldn't there be accord between the two? How do we even understand the text of Revelation without any employment of rational investigation? Should we not seek to provide rational answers to misconceptions about our creed? But again, what do we mean by reason? *A priori* knowledge? Does that even exist? If it does, is there an agreed-upon set of *a priori* information? Did the philosophers ever agree on much, other than what the rest of humanity have agreed upon using their philosophically unschooled intellects? Didn't their schooled intellects lead them to beliefs about the world we consider now totally

---

[18] El-Tobgui, *Reason, Revelation & the Reconstitution of Rationality,* 156.

absurd? In what do we ground our individual or group rational findings, and what guarantees their correctness? These and others are all valid questions that need answers in order to begin talking about the place of rational inquiry in metaphysics or the world of the unseen. While detailed answers are well beyond the scope of this paper, I will try to briefly address the main issues of contention here.

First, let us agree that subjecting the Divine instruction to the prevalent intellectual or social conventions is always a perilous undertaking. Take, for example, the Aristotelian concept of God. To Aristotle, God was the unmoved mover, who must be radically simple and changeless or undifferentiated and undifferentiating. He is pure actuality without any unactualized potential. This also meant that he does not do anything new at any time and that he does not exert influence on the universe as an efficient cause, but only as a final cause, meaning that the universe reacts to him without any action emanating from him. While this posed a problem for his followers who struggled to explain change in the universe, it may have been at some level fine for Aristotle, because his god is not a creator. Afterall, for him, matter was eternal without beginning, not a created thing. This Aristotelian concept of God, however, seems to come into irreconcilable conflict with the Quranic description of God, wherein He engages with His temporal creations, as He wills, while acknowledging that time itself is His creation, so He is not bound by it, just as He is not bound by space. Aristotelian and Neoplatonic philosophies prevailed in the new lands of Islam during its early spread. Muslim apologists worked hard to provide Islamic answers that could be accepted within the intellectual milieu of those times and places. Much controversy and division among Muslims resulted from this. Did we have to reconcile our understanding of the Quranic description of God and His voluntary actions with any Aristotelian or Neoplatonic dicta? We will come to see later why we did not need to, but do we ever have to engage with different intellectual paradigms?

First, at a more superficial level, using the technical language of a particular group of people, for example, the philosophers, should not be problematic when done by the astute debater who is well aware of the connotative power of terms and how undivorceable they are from their intellectual/social milieu. We find, in addition to the *Mutakallimeen* (rationalist theologians), scripturalists like Ibn Taymiyyah (rA) not shying away from using Avicennian terms such as *wâjib al-wujood* (necessary existent). In fact, Ibn Taymiyyah clearly states that there is no problem in adopting and adapting the technical language of different groups whenever the need arises.[19]-[viii]

---

[19] Ibn Taymiyyah, Taqi al-Deen Ahmad ibn 'Abd al-Ḥaleem, *Majmoo' al-Fatâwa*, 2nd ed., ed. 'Abd al-Raḥmân ibn Qâsim al-Najdi, 20 vols. (Cairo: Maktabat Ibn Taymiyyah, n.d.), 3:306.

Second, using the techniques of rational metaphysicians is different from using their technical language. The danger in using their techniques is obvious: we would be subjecting the Revelation to an outside philosophical system. However, to engage with their discourse, we must use their techniques. To not engage with it, we may leave the masses unarmed against the rational metaphysicians' propositions and attacks. Initially, the great faith the earlier generations had in their hearts and their firm establishment (*tamakkun*) in their spiritual experiences spared them from the temptation to pay attention to contenders, no matter how glittery their dialectics may have seemed. That is why we find an imam like Ahmad ibn Ḥanbal (rA) completely opposed to engaging in the discourse of speculative theologians and philosophers, and we all know how critical he was of the great traditional scholar, al-Ḥârith al-Muḥâsibi (rA), for engaging in their discourse. It seems, however, that many-and-later-most scholars from the fifth century onward have decided to engage with *kalâm* in order to defend the tradition. Atharis remained largely skeptical of *kalâm*. They felt that such engagement compromised the tradition and the collective consciousness of Muslims; so, to them, the harm outweighed any benefit. They continued to condemn *kalâm*, while the Mutakallimoon continued to condemn the literalism of the Atharis, and some of them would even call them *ḥashwiyyah* (or *ḥashawiyyah*), which is a pejorative term meaning that they relate too many reports without comprehending them, or that they are marginal and eccentric. Ibn Taymiyyah (rA) then came at a time when the intellectual idiom of the scholarly community and even of public space has been saturated with *kalâm*, so he decided to engage with it (thus the notion of him being a *mutakallim*). However, he did not do that in the way cotemporaneous speculative theologians did, but rather to defend the Athari dicta, which found their strongest patronage among the Ḥanbalis. He even explicitly permitted rational theological argument at some level and showed that it has first been employed by the Quran in his *al-khawḍ* fatwa, written in Egypt and included in the beginning of his magnum opus *Dar'*.[20]-ix While most Atharis appreciated his service of their cause, some, particularly during his time, were still skeptical of the mere engagement of *kalâm* and rational theology, something they felt Ahmad (rA) would have not accepted.

So, now, what do we do with *kalâm* and how do we engage with rational theology if we were to engage with it in the first place?

First, it must be emphasized that the different disciplines of philosophy, including logic, have undergone

---

[20] Ibn Taymiyyah, *Dar' Ta'âruḍ al-'Aql wa al-Naql*, 1:29.

massive changes. If we use an old philosophical discourse to address a modern audience, we would be doing a disservice to the religion and our "apologetics." The *kalâm* of the fourth, fifth, and sixth centuries AH was formulated to address a philosophical discourse, prevalent during those times, which underwent profound changes. Second, I believe there is room for using relevant rational arguments (*kalâm*) to defend our *'aqeedah*. I believe that what our great imams, like al-Shâfi'i and Ahmad, dispraised was making the revealed knowledge subordinate to *kalâm*. I believe that what caused Ibn Khuzaymah, Ibn Surayj, al-Harawi, Ibn 'Abd al-Barr, and other Atharis to be justifiably opposed to *kalâm* in their times is that they perceived that many established dicta of the Revelation were being reversed or altered in order to adjust the tradition to the requirements of certain philosophies. We must not feel the need to reconcile the revealed knowledge with an outside philosophy, because revealed knowledge is self-sufficient. We only need to reconcile our understanding of the revealed knowledge with the mental axioms, such as the Aristotelian formulated law of non-contradiction, as well as things perceptible by the senses. However, we must be aware that the science of logic is not infallible. Logicians have disagreed with each other since Aristotle's time. Anyone who has studied the development of logic over the centuries has no doubt about that. In this light, Imam Ibn

Taymiyyah's critique of *kalâm* should be understood. He was a master of the rational sciences to the point that some considered him to have prefigured the British empiricists and the nominalists. His critique was of some methodologies and assertions of the Greek philosophers. That is why I like the title *Ibn Taymiyya Against the Greek Logicians* that Wael B. Hallaq chose for his splendid translation of al-Suyooṭi's *Jahd al-Qareeḥah fi Tajreed al-Naṣeeḥah*, a summary of Ibn Taymiyyah's *Response to the Logicians* (*al-Radd 'Ala al-Manṭiqiyeen*).

It is understood that most people choose between the thesis and antithesis, but for those who are interested in synthesis, the following approach to *kalâm* may be the solution.

Let us imagine the theological discourse in two major steps:

1- Establishing the purports of the Revelation, our ultimate source of metaphysical knowledge.
2- Developing systematic rational arguments in defense of those purports, an endeavor that is closer to the discipline of apologetics than it is to the discipline of theology.[21]

---

[21] Hoover says about Ibn Taymiyyah, "In my analysis of *Ikhtiyāriyya*, I call him an 'apologist' seeking to elucidate and defend an 'ordinary language' reading of the theological data of revealed tradition as rational and coherent" (Jon Hoover, *Ibn Taymiyya's Theodicy of Perpetual Optimism* [Leiden: Brill, 2007], 22).

Does rational inquiry have a role in the first step? Well, it depends on what is meant by rational inquiry. If it is using reason as an independent source of metaphysical knowledge, then it does not, at least for people who were privileged by receiving a revelation and who have come to realize its Divine origin. We cannot accept rational molds and frameworks produced by a particular philosophical school and then attempt to fit the dictates of the Revelation into them. In this step, we will use our unadulterated reason to ascertain the reliability (*thuboot*) of reports and to understand their implications (*dalâlah*) through the linguistic conventions of the first community and their own understanding. Their understating should always be privileged because they were "the first audience," purest at heart, deepest in knowledge, and least pretentious or hyper-technical. Also, a hermeneutical system that places an emphasis on contextuality and intertextuality will never demand reason to resign or disengage it from any inquiry. This would, most importantly, be a betrayal of the Revelation's emphatic appeal to "reason" and "reflect."

In the second phase where we try to demonstrate the rational integrity of the Islamic doctrines, there is a much greater place for rational arguments to be employed. What is to be remembered here, however, is the limitation of the human mind and the human categories of thought. We must also remember that the complete dissimilarity between the *ghayb* and *shahâdah* makes drawing inferences about the former from the latter erroneous and dangerous. Finally, the absolute incomparability of God makes categorical syllogism (*qiyâs al-shumool*) and analogy (*qiyâs al-tamtheel*) inoperative in inferring from the creation about Him. Only, in a careful manner, may the *a fortiori* argument be employed to ascribe to God perfections found in His creations as long as they are completely clear of any imperfection.[22-x] The Prophet (pbuh) taught us how to apply the *a fortiori* argument to simplify things for the apprehension of the human mind. Abu Razeen al-'Uqayli, a Companion of the Prophet, reported:

> I asked the Prophet one day: "Will each and every one of us see our Lord on the Day of Resurrection? Is there a sign for this in the creation?" The Prophet answered: "Abu Razeen, the fact that each and every one of you sees the moon is in itself a sign for this, is it not?" I replied: "Of course." The Prophet said: "So, God is the greatest."[23-xi]

While this hadith may have a controversial transmission, it is not establishing anything new. The

[22] Ibn Taymiyyah, *Dar' Ta'âruḍ al-'Aql wa al-Naql*, 1:29.

[23] Reported by Ahmad, Abu Dâwood and others with a chain that is weak, but is subject to *taḥseen* (strengthening) by corroborative reports. Adapted from the translation in Holtzman, "Does God Really Laugh?", 165-200, https://doi.org/10.1515/9783110245486.165.

Prophet (pbuh) said in a report that is related by both al-Bukhari and Muslim:

"إِنَّكُمْ سَتَرَوْنَ رَبَّكُمْ كَمَا تَرَوْنَ هَذَا الْقَمَرَ لَا تُضَامُونَ فِي رُؤْيَتِهِ"

> "You will see your Lord as you see this full moon, and you will have no trouble in seeing Him."

Seeing the Lord on the Day of Judgment is a matter of agreement among Ahl al-Sunnah. The Prophet (pbuh) is not likening God to the moon, but likening the ease of our seeing God on the Day of Judgment to the ease of our seeing the moon in this life.

Finally, to say that the fence between the two steps mentioned above can be made completely impermeable is ahistorical, if not completely irrational. Therefore, we must remember that engaging rational theology will never be without risks. Ibn Taymiyyah (rA) quotes Abu Bakr ibn al-'Arabi (rA) as saying: "Our shaykh [al-Ghazâli] penetrated into the guts of philosophers, then he wanted to come back out, but could not."[24]-[xii] Others claimed that Ibn Taymiyyah himself was also affected by his mastery of philosophy. While this Athari writer agrees more with Ibn Taymiyyah on epistemology and theology, and believes that his Atharism often helped him, it is untenable to categorically deny that claim. Should we then favor safety? It may not be possible given how dire our need is to

---

[24] Ibn Taymiyyah, *Dar' Ta'âruḍ al-'Aql wa al-Naql*, 1:5.

engage with the dominant intellectual idiom of our times. However, we must exercise extreme caution, because if Ḥujjat al-Islam and Shaykh al-Islam could not cross that ocean without getting wet, who can? Muslim apologists of all persuasions had to engage with different intellectual paradigms in order to defend our Islamic doctrines. They still do. We should scrutinize their legacies through the sieve of the Quran, the Sunnah, and the understanding of the first community, all while understanding their noble motivation and preserving their sacred honor.

Before I move to addressing the notion of a conflict between reason and Revelation, let me briefly discuss the role of two major concepts in our epistemic theory: *fiṭrah* and *ilhâm*.

The Role of *Fiṭrah*

"عن وابِصَةَ بنِ مَعْبَدٍ رضي الله عنه: أتيتُ رسولَ اللهِ – صلى الله عليه وسلم – فقال: جِئْتَ تَسْأَلُ عَنِ الْبِرِّ. قُلْتُ: نَعَمْ. قال: اسْتَفْتِ قَلْبَكَ؛ الْبِرُّ مَا اطْمَأَنَّتْ إِلَيْهِ النَّفْسُ وَاطْمَأَنَّ إِلَيْهِ الْقَلْبُ، وَالإِثْمُ مَا حَاكَ فِي النَّفْسِ وَتَرَدَّدَ فِي الصَّدْرِ وَإِنْ أَفْتَاكَ النَّاسُ وَأَفْتَوْكَ."

Wâbiṣah ibn Ma'bad (rA) said: I came to the Messenger of Allah (pbuh) and he said, "You

> have come to ask about righteousness." I said, "Yes." He said, "Consult your heart. Righteousness is that about which the soul feels at ease and the heart feels tranquil, and *ithm* (sin) is that which wavers in the soul and causes uneasiness in the chest, even though people have repeatedly given their fatwa (expert opinion)."[25]

The difficulty in talking about *fiṭrah* starts from the very translation of the word, which has been translated as: natural constitution, original disposition, natural inclination, original normative disposition, and so forth.

The relationship between *fiṭrah* and reason is a complicated one. While *fiṭrah* has been used in the tradition to refer to *a priori* knowledge, it is not limited to the intellect, but it is the general normative disposition of the human intellect that helps us to apprehend *a priori* facts and compelling (*ḍaroori*) knowledge, and it is also the original disposition of the heart and the human psyche. It is not only about knowledge, but about feelings as well. It is not only about knowing what is right, but also about choosing it. We were created in the best shape

---

[25] Reported by Ahmad and al-Dârimi through a sound chain.

(*aḥsan taqweem*), both externally and internally. The Prophet relates from Allah that He said,

"وَإِنِّي خَلَقْتُ عِبَادِي حُنَفَاءَ كُلَّهُمْ"

> "I have created all My servants having a natural inclination to uprightness (the worship of the One God)." [Muslim]

But how do we use the *fiṭrah* when humans are always disagreeing over what some of them consider *fiṭri* (innate)? In dialectics, *fiṭrah* should be invoked only when there is human concurrence (*tawâtur*). That consensus of human beings on accepting a certain notion is an indication that it is built into our *fiṭrah*. The law of non-contradiction is an example of something humans would agree on. It is not limited to mental axioms: the superiority of kindness over cruelty, for instance, is another. Praise God, there are still matters that people endowed with reason do agree on.

There is another problem with *fiṭrah* even for our personal pursuit of the truth. It is corruptible. While Ibn Taymiyyah (rA) gave *fiṭrah* a prominent place in his epistemological theory, contrary to what some of his detractors may think, he was well aware of its corruptibility. In fact, he mentions seven of its fatal diseases: *hawa* (bias), *ẓann* (conjecture), *shubhah* (misgiving), *gharad* (ulterior motive), *'âdah* (habit), *taqleed* (blind following), *mawrooth* (inherited beliefs).[26] He mentions how spiritual refinement (*riyâdah*) through devotion and *'ibâdah* (worship) along with immersion in the Revelation are important to rehabilitating our *fiṭrah*. This would bring us to the role of *ilhâm* (inspiration), which not only rescues the *fiṭrah*, but goes far beyond that.

The place of *ilhâm*

There are many layers or degrees of *ilhâm* in our Sufi vernacular. It will suffice here to talk about the general concept. It is well known that toward the end of his life, Imam al-Ghazâli (rA) placed *mushâhadât al-haqâ'iq* (the apprehension of realities) through spiritual disclosure (*kashf*) at the top of the epistemological pyramid, arguing that true certainty can only be gained through it, and at the same time he downplayed the utility of *kalâm*. You find this in his *al-Munqidh min al-Ḍalâl* (Deliverer from Error) and other books. He says in *Ihyâ' 'Uloom al-Deen*,

> the middle path (*ḥadd al-iqtiṣâd*) between the "wantonness" (*inḥilâl*) of excessive *ta'weel* [of the philosophers] and the "rigidity (*jumood*) of the

[26] El-Tobgui, *Reason, Revelation & the Reconstitution of Rationality*, 284.

> Ḥanbalites" is a fine and subtle [point] comprehensible only to those who have been granted success and who perceive things by a divine light, not by means of receiving transmitted knowledge (*samâʿ*). Then, when the hidden aspects of things are made manifest to them as they truly are, they consider the transmitted texts [of Revelation] and the wording thereof, and whatever agrees with what they have witnessed by the light of certainty, they affirm it, and whatever disagrees with this, they reinterpret it.[27-xiii]

While we may disagree with the hierarchy mentioned by Imam al-Ghazâli (rA), we recognize that, while *ilhâm* must be subordinated to the text of Revelation, its complementary utility is undeniable. After all, Allah says,

﴿وَاتَّقُوا اللَّهَ ۖ وَيُعَلِّمُكُمُ اللَّهُ ۗ وَاللَّهُ بِكُلِّ شَيْءٍ عَلِيمٌ﴾

> "And fear Allah. And Allah teaches you." [Al-Baqarah 2:282]

In Livnat Holtzman's words,

> According to Ibn al-Qayyim, the knowledge of God's attributes cannot be obtained by the human intellect alone and should not be acquired for mere

---

[27] Abu Ḥâmid Muhammad ibn Muhammad al-Ghazâli, *Iḥyâ' ʿUloom al-Deen* (Beirut: Dâr al-Maʿrifah, n.d.), 1:104. Translation adapted from El-Tobgui, *Reason, Revelation & the Reconstitution of Rationality,* 126.

intellectual purposes. Rather, the knowledge of God's attributes is the outcome of a spiritual labor, in which God participates actively by widening or opening the believer's heart to receive the meaning of the attributes. The heart therefore receives this knowledge directly from the niche of divine inspiration (*mishkât al-waḥy*).[28]

'Â'ishah (rAa) reported Allah's Messenger (pbuh) as saying:

"قَدْ كَانَ فِي الأُمَمِ قَبْلَكُمْ مُحَدَّثُونَ فَإِنْ يَكُنْ فِي أُمَّتِي مِنْهُمْ أَحَدٌ فَإِنَّ عُمَرَ بْنَ الْخَطَّابِ مِنْهُمْ."

"There had been among the people before

you inspired persons (*muḥaddathoon*), and if

there were any such among my Ummah,

'Umar b. al-Khaṭṭâb would be one of them."

(Agreed upon)

'Umar (rAa) never used his inspiration as an independent source of knowledge about God, but only as a means to a better understanding of the intent of God in His Revelation.

I hope that it has become clear that spiritual labor is of utmost importance to rehabilitate the *fiṭrah* and be worthy of receiving guidance (or *ilhâm*) from Allah.

---

[28] Holtzman, "Accused of Anthropomorphism," 561-587.

What If There Is a Conflict Between Reason and Revelation?

Imam Mâlik (rA) said,

"أَوَ كُلَّمَا جَاءَنَا رَجُلٌ أَجْدَلُ مِنْ رَجُلٍ تَرَكْنَا مَا جَاءَ بِهِ
جِبْرِيلُ عليه السلام على مُحَمَّدٍ – صلى الله عليه وسلم – لِجَدَلِهِ؟"

> Shall we, whenever a man comes to us more argumentative than another, abandon what Jibreel (pbuh) has brought to Muhammad (pbuh) for his argumentation? (Reported by Abu Nu'aym in *al-Ḥilyah*)

We have talked about the primacy of the Revelation, but we also talked about the distinguished place the Revelation itself assigns to reason. What if they conflict?

Various answers have been posited by different prominent figures in our intellectual history. For some of the philosophers, reconciliation was achieved by creating what may be considered a theory of a two-fold truth, where philosophy and Revelation accord with each other but speak at different levels. Al-Farâbi, for instance, saw the language of Revelation as a popular expression of truth in figurative terms that is suitable for the philosophically unschooled intellects.[29] Ibn Rushd (rA), says, "Those things which cannot be known except in demonstration (*burhân*), because of their concealment, God was kind

[29] Deborah L.Black, "Al-Farabi," in *History of Islamic Philosophy*, eds, Seyyed Hossein Nasr and Oliver Leaman, 178-197 (London & New York: Routledge), 2001,181.

enough with His servants who are not able to understand by demonstration... and has given those *amthâl* (similes, examples, or analogies) and called them to believe them."[30-xiv] Ibn Rushd insisted that there is complete harmony between religion and philosophy, but at two different levels: philosophy addresses those capable of understanding demonstrative discourse, while religion uses rhetorical language that can be understood by the masses and thus benefit them. This two-fold truth was the hallmark of Averroism that thrived in Europe for centuries and was adopted by philosophers like Siger of Brabant and Boetius of Dacia, although later condemned by the church and considered particularly dangerous by Thomas Aquinas.

It would be unfair to exaggerate in condemning Ibn Rushd's notion of a twofold truth. Different explanations of the claimed conflict between Revelation and reason have been suggested, some by imams who are considered more "traditional" than he is. Al-Taftazâni (rA) says,

> If it is said, if the correct religious belief is the negation of spatial locatedness and directionality, why is it then that the heavenly scriptures and the

---

[30] Abu al-Waleed Muhammad ibn Ahmad Ibn Rushd, *Faṣl al-Maqâl wa-Taqreer ma bayn al-Ḥikmah wa al-Sharee'ah min Ittiṣâl*, 2nd ed., ed. Muhammad 'Umârah (Cairo: Dar al-Ma ârif, n.d.), 46. Translation from Ajhar A. Hakim, "The Forgotten Rational Thinking in the Ḥanbalite Thought With Special Reference to Ibn Taymiyya," *Journal of Arabic and Islamic Studies* 14, no. 1 (2014): 137, https://doi.org/10.5617/jais.4642.

> Prophetic traditions imply in countless instances the affirmation of that without a single instance of negating it? The answer is: because exoneration from directionality is something the intellects of the masses cannot comprehend, to the extent that they would be certain that something that does not exist in any direction does not exist at all. [Therefore,] a discourse with apparent assimilation (*tashbeeh*) was more suitable in addressing them and calling them to the religion, and more conducive to their uprightness.[31-xv]

It seems, at least to this writer, that the two-fold truth of Ibn Rushd (rA) is a cleverer explanation of what appears to some as a conflict.

For Atharis, the most that can be said is that there is only one Truth about the unseen, and that it was expressed by the Revelation in a manner that suits all audiences and a language that all could relate to, particularly the first audience entrusted with the first enactment of the religious doctrines. This language is still anthropic, conforming to the human categories of understanding, because the audience is humanity. The Revelation used the language developed by humans[32] to

---

[31] Sa'd al-Deen Mas'ood ibn 'Umar al-Taftazâni, *Sharḥ al-Maqâṣid*, ed. Ibrâheem Shams al-Deen (Beirut: Dâr al-Kutub al-'Ilmiyyah, 2010), 3:36.

[32] This is based on the stronger position that languages mostly evolved through human usage to express things and concepts in their environments. See Ibn Taymiyyah, *Majmoo' al-Fatâwa*, 7:90-96, for a

denote things and concepts within their experience in order to point to things and concepts whose realities are beyond human apprehension. That is why in Sufi terminology the concept of "borrowed names" (*al-ism al-mu'âr*) is often used.

Addressing the notion of a conflict between the Revelation and reason more directly and in greater detail, Imam Fakhr al-Din al-Râzi (rA) speaks in *Asâs al-Taqdees* of what he calls a "universal law" (*qanoon kulli*), which is summarized as:

> If the obvious outward meaning of the revealed texts and the definitive conclusions of rational thought are in conflict, then either: (1) they must both be accepted, which is impossible as this would violate the law of non-contradiction [claiming both *p* and *p*]; (2) they must both be rejected, which is also impossible as this would violate the law of the excluded middle [claiming neither *p* nor *p*]; (3) precedence must be given to Revelation, which is impossible since Revelation is grounded in reason, such that if we were to give priority to the former over the latter [that is, to Revelation over reason], this would amount to a rejection of both reason and

detailed discussion on whether languages are *iṣṭilâḥi* (developed by humans) or *tawqeefi* (revealed by God). He argues it is not a case of excluded middle, and shows that the faculty was created by God, and some "names" were taught to Adam by God, but languages were mostly developed over time by humans, who were assisted by divine inspiration.

[by extension] that which is grounded by reason [i.e., Revelation]. One must, therefore, give precedence to reason, then either make figurative interpretation (*ta'weel*) of scripture [to accord with reason], or negate the apparent meaning of scripture but refrain from assigning to it a definite, particular, metaphorical meaning (*tafweeḍ*).[33-xvi]

Ibn Taymiyyah agreed with Ibn Rushd on the complete harmony between reason and Revelation. He did not accept philosophy as a spokesperson for reason, and he did not accept the notion of two layers of truth. He rejected al-Râzi's universal law, and he provided in a ten-volume tome his alternative. In the following paragraphs, I will briefly go over some of his main points:

- Ibn Taymiyyah (rA) did not attempt to belittle the office of reason or deny its importance in grounding our faith in the Revelation.
- He argued that reason is not one undifferentiated category of conclusive (*qaṭ'i*) rational output. He argued that most rational propositions are speculative (*ẓanni*) and they naturally should not be given precedence over the conclusive assertions

[33] Fakhr al-Deen al-Râzi, *Asâs al-Taqdees,* ed. Ahmad Hijâzi al-Saqâ (Cairo: Maktabat al-Kulliyyât al-Azhariyyah, 1406/1986), 220. Translation adapted from El-Tobgui, *Reason, Revelation & the Reconstitution of Rationality,* 133-134.

of the Revelation. The same applies to the Revelation, so it would be natural that we give precedence to what is conclusive, regardless of whether it is rational or scriptural. When they are both *ẓanni*, we look for the more probative (*râjiḥ*) proofs. There is, thus, no simple binary of reason versus Revelation.

- If it is said that al-Râzi (rA) was only talking about conclusive indicants of reason, Ibn Taymiyyah (rA) denied that they ever conflicted with the obvious implications of the Revelation. He argued that most of what al-Râzi seems to consider conclusive is not in fact so. He maintained that the established findings of sense perception (*ḥiss*) and *a priori* (*badeehi*) reason can never be ignored in favor of Revelation, but they also never needed to be ignored because the Revelation never contradicted them. A conflict between the conclusive deliverances of these three sources of knowledge is simply impossible.
- Ibn Taymiyyah argued that reason testified to the veracity of the Revelation in its entirety, which is proven by miracles in addition to other signs of its Divine origin. Contrarily, the Revelation did not deem rational propositions all true. If one must be given precedence, it should be the Revelation.

However, the conflict between the conclusive proofs of both is inconceivable and non-existent; hence, there is no need to resort to *tarjeeḥ* (favoring one).

- He talked about the philosophers diverging among themselves on everything, much more so than did the followers of the three heavenly religions. He mentioned that their disagreements on the arithmetic knowledge of astronomy is greater than the disagreements among the different Muslim sects. The reason that is definitive is only the *badeehi* knowledge that is accepted by human concurrence (*tawâtur*), not the ruminations of the graduates of a particular philosophical school or intellectual elites that are perpetually conflicted among themselves.
- While he agreed on reason grounding the Revelation, Ibn Taymiyyah also argued that the opposite is true, because the Revelation salvages reason from the many flaws that would otherwise undercut its utility, such as bias, vanity, arrogance, ulterior motives, partisanship, and the like.

Accepting anything as definitive simply because the majority of the intellectual elites uphold it is unfounded and dangerous. There are many Islamic creeds and practices that would be questioned on that basis. Also, what is considered counter to reason by the formulators of the universal law is not a matter of agreement among "reasonable" people. For example, Ibn Rushd, the great jurist and the most celebrated philosopher in Islamic history, denied that God's aboveness (*'uluw*), which is said to mean directionality (*jihah*), necessitates corporealism. This was one ring in a chain that led many rationalist theologians to deny the aboveness of God. Are we to believe that the "Commentator" is not intelligent enough to apprehend a conclusive proof of reason? Also, the proof of origination of accidents (*ḥudooth al-a'râḍ*) as evidence on the origination of the world did not convince the vast majority of philosophers.

Egalitarian Epistemology

Should there be two sets of beliefs in the foundations of the religion?

We have seen how the philosophers talked about a two-fold truth and the language of the Revelation being intentionally figurative for the apprehension of the masses. This was not limited to the philosophers. Many of the *kalâm* theologians in the caliber of Imams al-'Izz, al-Taftazâni, al-Haytami and al-Sanoosi maintained that most people are corporealists (*mujassimah*) because they believe in directionality (*jihah*) among other primary meanings of the text of Revelation. They mostly did not hereticate them, even though most of them consider those views *kufr* (disbelief). They would even cite the hadith of the girl who, when asked by the Prophet, "Where is Allah?"

answered, "Above the heavens." They would also mention as justification for not excommunicating them that the primary meanings of the text all tend toward this interpretation, whereas the proofs to the contrary are extremely subtle and difficult.[34]

Here are some concerns, shared by Imam Abu al-Muzaffar al-Sam'âni (rA), about subjecting our beliefs to rational inquiry and the resultant epistemological disparity, as approvingly quoted by Imam Ibn Ḥajar (rA),

> Abu al-Muzaffar ibn al-Sam'âni cited the verses and hadiths of this chapter[35] to prove the invalidity of the way of the *Mutakallimeen* (rationalist theologians) in the classification of things into body, substance, and accident... "...they rely on their conjecture and what their rational inquiry leads them to, and then they subject the texts of revelation to it; whatever is consistent with it, they accept it, and whatever is in conflict with it, they reject it." He [Abu al-Muzaffar] then quoted these

---

[34] Ibn 'Abd al-Salâm, *Qawâ'id al-Aḥkâm*, 1:201-202; al-Taftazâni, *Sharḥ al-Maqâṣid*, 3:36; Ahmad ibn Muhammad ibn Ḥajar al-Haytami, *Tuḥfat al-Muḥtâj fi Sharḥ al-Minhâj* (Cairo: al-Maktabah al-Tijâriyyah al-Kubrâ, 1357/1983), 9:86; Muhammad ibn Yoosuf al-Sanoosi, *Sharḥ al-'Aqeedah al-Kubra*, ed. al-Sayyid Yoosuf Ahmad (Beirut: Dâr al-Kutub al-'Ilmiyyah, 2006), 62.

[35] Chapter on the saying of Allah, "O Messenger, announce that which has been revealed to you from your Lord, and if you do not, then you have not conveyed His message."

verses and their likes containing the command to convey [the message]. He said, "of this that was required to be conveyed is *tawḥeed*; in fact, it is the foundation of all commands; so, he (pbuh) did not leave a matter of the affairs of this *deen*, whether it is its foundations, maxims, or legislations, except that he (pbuh) conveyed it. He (pbuh) did not leave out anything except what they cite of the 'substance' and 'accident,' and there is not a single utterance traceable to him (pbuh) or any of his Companions in this respect. It is, therefore, evident that they sought a way other than theirs and took a path other than theirs, which is an innovated, fabricated path that is different from that of the Messenger (pbuh) and his Companions (may Allah be pleased with them). Taking that path would inevitably lead to deriding and discrediting the *salaf* and ascribing to them lack of knowledge and confusion. So, beware of engaging with their *kalâm* or paying attention to their propositions, for they are incoherent and self-contradictory ... To appreciate the ugliness of the necessary concomitants of their way, it is sufficient for you [to note] that if we were to agree with their propositions and require them of the people, it becomes necessary to excommunicate all of the [Muslim] public, because they know not except

> absolute compliance. If this path were to be presented to them, their majority would not understand it, let alone become fully aware of its basis. Instead, the extent of their [the public's] *tawḥeed* is abiding by what they found their imams in the creeds of the *deen* to uphold, holding on to it with their molars, and adhering to the functions of worship and remembrance with hearts that are sound and clear of doubts; so, you find them unwilling to turn away from what they believed, even if they were to be cut up in pieces. So, let them rejoice in this certainty, and glad tidings be to them for staying within this safety. If these have committed disbelief, and they are the mainstream and vast majority of this Ummah, then that would lead to nothing short of undoing Islam and destroying the minaret of the *deen*." And Allah is the one we beseech for help.[36]-[xvii]

While it is true that many of the details of the religion may be beyond the comprehension of the masses, it is inconceivable that foundational matters about God's

---

[36] Ibn Ḥajar al-'Asqalâni, *Fatḥ al-Bâri fi Sharḥ Ṣaḥeeḥ al-Bukhâri* (Beirut: Dâr al-Ma'rifah, 1959), 13:507. It is clear from this quotation that the binary division of the scholars into *Atharis* and *Mutakallimeen* is not absolute. Where do we now place Ibn Ḥajar? He would sometimes make *ta'weel* of the attributes that is more consistent with the way of the *Mutakallimeen*. Does that make him of them? Can we say that in light of this quotation and others like it?

attributes should be subject to a tiered system of belief, with the public being led by the text of Revelation to believing in what is in reality a clear matter of disbelief. Yaḥya Michot explained that Imam Ibn Taymiyyah fought to uphold "the self-sufficiency of the religious rationality manifested in scriptural literality and common faith, and its validity for all, the elite and the crowd."[37]

[37] J. Yahya Michot, "A Mamlūk Theologian's Commentary on Avicenna's *Risāla Aḍḥawiyya*, being a translation of a part of the *Dar' al-Ta'āruḍ* of Ibn Taymiyya, with introduction, annotation, and appendices." *Journal of Islamic Studies* 14, no. 2 (2003): 149–203, 171.

A TYPOLOGY OF ISLAMIC POSITIONS ON THE ATTRIBUTES OF GOD

Negative theology in Islam is said to have started with al-Ja'd ibn Dirham[38] but was effectively propagated by al-Jahm ibn Safwân,[39] thus the title "Jahmi" is sometimes liberally applied to all shades of negationists. The roots of this innovation are not agreed upon among the researchers, but there are three main theories: Neoplatonic, Buddhist, or Christian-patristic.[40]

Providing a comprehensive typology of the positions of Muslims concerning the Divine names and attributes mentioned in the scriptures is well beyond the scope of

---

[38] Al-Ja'd ibn Dirham was the teacher of Jahm b. Ṣafwân; they lived during the reign of the Umayyad caliph Marwân II, in the second century AH.

[39] Jahm ibn Ṣafwân was strongly criticized for his doctrines by later scholars. Imams Ahmad, al-Bukhari, and al-Dârimi all wrote refutations of Jahm's theological positions.

[40] Michael Chase, "From the four Aristotelian questions to *tawḥīd*: Notes on the origins of negative theology in Islam," retrieved from https://www.academia.edu/39185335/From_the_four_Aristotelian_questions_to_tawḥīd_Notes_on_the_origins_of_negative_theology_in_Islam

this work. Not only that there are countless groups, but within each group there are innumerable shades of interpretations. What is provided here is a crude division of the main positions and groups to allow us to have a bird's-eye view of the entire field before we embark on delineating the Athari position according to this writer. To have an objective classification of the positions adopted by Muslims concerning the Divine names and attributes, I will start from the most negationist to the most affirmationist, keeping in mind that describing some extremists as affirmationists is merely for the sake of simplification. This does not mean that likening Allah to His creations or inventing modalities of His attributes are parts of affirmation; they are not. They are simply deviations. Note also that the titles in this classification are mine, and they are meant to simplify the matter.

I. Absolute Negationists (*Mu'aṭṭilah*)

Negationism (*nafy*) is also referred to as *ta'ṭeel* (stripping God of His attributes), which, in the case of absolute negationism, leads to turning God into a merely abstract principle of no ontological reality, completely unknowable, and thus completely unapproachable. *Nafy* and *ta'ṭeel* are the closest terms in our tradition to apophatism and negative theology.

This position is attributed to the Qarmatians.[41] They refer to God only via the negative, so they would not even say that He exists, but they would rather say that he does not not exist.[42] This stance is not only limited to Qarmatians, however. In his paper, "Unsaying God," Aydogan Kars quotes the following translation of the Ismaelite scholar Abu Tammâm's description of some Zaydis' position on the Divine attributes:

> These people will not describe God with any description that is suitable for created things nor will they say of Him that He is either knowing [*ālim*] or not not knowing [*lā lā ʿālim*], not powerful [*lā qādir*] or not not powerful [*lā lā qādir*], not a thing [*lā shayʾ*] or not not a thing [*lā lā shayʾ*], not confined [*lā maḥdūd*] or not not confined [*lā lā maḥdūd*]. They speak about the creator neither on the basis of reality nor through metaphor. They rather talk by approximation [*taqrīb*]. Thus, if they were asked about God, "do you recognize Him?" they would remain silent. They will not say that we recognize Him [*naʿrifuhu*] or that we do not not recognize Him [*lā lā naʿrifuhu*]. For them, if they were to recognize Him, their recognition of Him

---

[41] This is a group of Isma'ilite Shi'ites who were also called Bâṭinites because of their esoteric interpretations of the texts that have no connection at all to their apparent meanings.

[42] al-Juwayni, *al-Irshâd* (Thaqâfah), 42.

> would encompass Him. Whoever is recognized and becomes recognizable to his recognizer cannot be a god.[43]

Many Muslim philosophers can be added to this group, albeit with some differences, because while they denied the Divine attributes, they still described the Divine as the necessary existent (*wâjib al-wujood*), or the nous (*'aql*), or some other descriptions.

One might add at this level some of the mystics of the philosophical Sufi tradition. However, those mystics had a composite position of complete negation and pantheistic affirmation, so while they negate all attributes of the ineffable ipseity (*dhât*), they affirm all Divine attributes to all of existence, which is, to them, nothing other than the Divine. This can be observed in Ibn Sab'een's statement,

عين ما ترى ذات لا ترى – وذات لا ترى عين ما ترى

> You see nothing other than the unseen ipseity – and the unseen ipseity is nothing other than what you see.[44]

To all in this group, the ineffable God is too great to be recognizable. While they may be the closest to negative theology, they still did not meet the strictest definition of

---

[43] Aydogan Kars, "Unsaying God," 2019. The researcher referenced Abu Tammâm, *Kitâb al-Shajarah*, 96 (Arabic text).

[44] Shams al-Deen Muhammad ibn Ahmad al-Dhahabi, *Al-'Arsh* (Madinah: Islamic University, 1424/2003), 1:91.

it, because they would still claim to know some aspects of theology apart from God.[45]

II. Relative Negationists (*Mu'aṭṭilah*)

The Mu'tazilah are the main protagonists of this group, and this position was then adopted by others, including most Twelvers, Ibadis, Zaydis, and even Ibn Ḥazm. But again, the Mu'tazilah, like all other groups have shades of understanding and the differences among them are numerous.

They generally accept the Divine names as proper names, but they deny the attributes (extant qualities) these names refer to, so they would accept the name *'Aleem*, but without the attribute of *'ilm* (knowledge). In fact, some of them say that there is no difference at all between *'Aleem* and *Qadeer*. Others say they are not the same, but still deny that they mean the corresponding attributes of *'ilm* and *qudrah* (power). They are mainly concerned about the problem of *tarkeeb* (composition). According to this philosophical argument, God must be radically simple and undifferentiated. If the attributes are distinct from the *dhât* (ipseity), then God is composed of the (*dhât*) and those attributes, which is a violation of *tawḥeed* (monism) according to them. Allah, then, knows, not by His knowledge, but by His *dhât* (ipseity), because

[45] Aydogan Kars, "Unsaying God," 2019.

he has no knowledge distinct from His ipseity. The Mu'tazilah are farther away from negative theology than the first group because their negation of the attributes is grounded in what they consider knowledge about God.

III. Relative Affirmationists

This group is represented by the latter Ash'aris and the Maturidis (*mâtureedi*). While there may be some differences between them, they largely agree on affirming the following attributes knowable through reason (*al-ṣifât al -'aqliyyah*), which are:

- One essential (*nafsiyyah*) attribute of existence
- Five negative (*salbiyyah*) attributes: these are the attributes of *qidam* (pre-eternity, which means He has no beginning), *al-baqâ'* (eternity without end), *waḥdâniyyah* (oneness, which means having no partner), *al-ghinâ'* (self-sufficiency, which means lack of need), *mukhâlafat al-ḥawâdith* (dissimilarity to originated things)
- Seven attributes of *ma'an* (qualities): these are the attributes of (*al-ḥayâh*) life, (*al-'ilm*) knowledge, (*al-irâdah*) will, (*al-qudrah*) power, (*al-sam'*) hearing, (*al-baṣar*) sight, (*al-kalâm*) speech

They believed that all these attributes are *qadeem* (pre-eternal) and they subsist in God.

They denied the "revealed attributes" (*al-ṣifât al-khabariyyah*) that they found to be rationally objectionable, like love, mercy, anger, the face, the hands, and the like. They also denied the "volitional attributes" (*al-ṣifât al-ihktiyâriyyah*), like instigating any action at a certain time, speaking, coming, descending to the lower heaven, and so forth. They were concerned about likening God to His creation and they were also concerned about violating some philosophical arguments they believed to be unchallengeable, such as the impossibility of a succession of temporally originating events (*ta'âqub al-ḥawâdith*) to subsist within the Divine.

Among the latter Ash'aris, the way they deal with the apparent meanings of the attributes they find rationally objectionable is by *ta'weel* (reinterpretation) or *tafweeḍ* (consigning its meaning to God).

IV. Predominantly Affirmationists

This group includes the earlier Ash'aris and their predecessors, like Ibn Kullâb (rA) and al-Qalânisi (rA).

Imam Abu al-Ḥasan al-Ash'ari (rA) and his most noble followers al-Bâqillâni (rA) and Ibn Furak (rA) affirmed the revealed attributes, including God's face, hand, and that He is above the Throne. They denied the volitional attributes for the concern about *ta'âqub al-ḥawâdith*.

This stance, which is heavily affirmationist except for the volitional attributes, continued to be the position of the followers of Abu al-Ḥasan al-Ash'ari until the time of Imam Abu al-Ma'âli al-Juwayni (rA) who negated the revealed attributes and adopted first *ta'weel* in his book *al-Irshâd*, and later *tafweeḍ* in *al-'Aqeedah al-Nizâmiyyah*, where he denounced *ta'weel* as something the *salaf*[46] (predecessors) unanimously avoided and did not consider *sâ'igh* (excusable).[47]

V. Affirmationists

This group may be called Atharis. Some may call them Ḥanbali or Ahl al-Ḥadith (Ḥadith scholars), but that may imply that Atharism is limited to these two groups, which is untrue. Their position will be discussed in detail later. They affirm all the attributes mentioned in the Quran and the Sunnah without assimilation (*tashbeeh*) or likening (*tamtheel*) God to His creations, and without alteration (*taḥreef*) or stripping (*ta'ṭeel*) God of His attributes.

To this author, some of the people of this group may have at times exceeded the bounds of proper affirmation

---

[46] Literally "predecessors," but in this context and in Islamic discourse generally, understood to be short for *al-salaf al-ṣâliḥ* (the righteous predecessors).

[47] Abu al-Ma'âli 'Abd al-Malik al-Juwayni, *Al-'Aqeedah al-Nizâmiyyah*, ed. M. Zâhid al-Kawthari (Cairo: al-Maktabah al-Azhariyyah lil-Turâth, 1412H), 31.

and breached the principle of *tanzeeh* (God's transcendence and incomparability), but these were rare and isolated incidents. The following groups are largely extinct, but they have had a significant presence in periods of our history, albeit without ever being a mainstream force.

VI. Extreme Affirmationists

This group includes Karrâmites, the followers of Muhammad ibn Karrâm (rA). These people are not one group, but they rather come in multiple shades, with some of them closer to Atharis than others. Some of them said that Allah is *jism/jawhar* (substance), only to negate that He is an *'arad* (accident), because of the Aristotelian categories being prevalent during those times in Muslim lands. According to Aristotle, existents may be either substance or accident. Since accidents are not self-subsistent and can only be predicated of or in some substance, then God must not be an accident, they argued. Allah did not describe Himself in these terms, so we must not. Additionally, it is claimed that they maintained that the attributes of God can come to exist at some point, so He may be described by an attribute after he was not. This is also a violation of the Sunni view that the species of any attribute is always *qadeem* and cannot be said to originate at a certain time. Only the actualization of individual manifestations of such attributes may be described to happen in succession, according to the Athari view. Some of them were so extreme in describing God and giving a modality (*kayf*) to His attributes that they talked about His *mumâssah* (touching) of the Throne.

VII. Assimilationists (*Mushabbihah*)

We could not put this group on the spectrum of affirmationists at all, because their deviation precludes them from even being called extreme affirmationists. While one may imagine the motives and the basis of the deviation of extreme affirmationists, one may not be able to extend the same understanding to assimilationists.

This group is represented by some of the early Twelvers, like Hishâm ibn al-Ḥakam (although there are conflicting reports about him), and Bayâniyyah (the followers of Bayân ibn Sam'ân) and individuals like Dâwood al-Jawareebi. Some accused Muqâtil ibn Sulaymân, the great exegete, of fitting into this group, but Ibn Taymiyyah said he was probably not this extreme.

WHAT DO WE BELIEVE IN?

There are many statements that capture the essence of Atharism (scripturalism) of which I will mention some.

Imam Ibn ʻAbd al-Barr (rA) said,

> The people of al-Sunnah unanimously agree on the affirmation of all the attributes that are in the Quran and the Sunnah and their being literal (*ḥaqeeqah*), not metaphorical (*majâz*), but they do not ascribe a modality to any of that and do not qualify them by a particular limiting description. As for the people of innovation, the Jahmiyyah, all of the Muʻtazilah, and the Kharijites, they all deny them and do not accept them as literal, and claim that those who accept them are anthropomorphists; and they are, to those who affirm them, negators of the worshiped Lord. The truth is in what the affirmers have said about what is stated in the Book of Allah and the Sunnah of His Messenger, and they are the imams of the Jamâʻah (the mainstream group), and to Allah is all praise.[48]-[xviii]

Sulṭân al-Awliyâ' Abdul-Qâdir al-Jilâni (rA) said,

---

[48] Ibn ʻAbd al-Barr, *Al-Tamheed,* 7:145.

We believe that Allah *yaqbiḍ* (constricts), *yabsuṭ* (expands), *yafraḥ* (rejoices), *yuḥibb* (loves), *yakrah* (dislikes), *yarḍâ* (becomes pleased), *yaghḍab* (becomes angry), and *yaskhaṭ* (abhors). He has two hands, and both of His hands are right. The hearts of the servants are between two of His fingers, and he is in the direction of *'uluw* (aboveness), *mustawin* (established) on the Throne, *muḥtawin* (encompassing). The Prophet (pbuh) approved the belief of the girl when he asked her, "Where is Allah?" and she pointed to the heavens… The attribute of *istiwâ'* (ascension/establishment) must be acknowledged without reinterpretation (*ta'weel*). It is the settling of His ipseity (*dhât*) above the Throne: not in the form of sitting and touching as the corporealists and Karrâmites have said, not in the form of high status and greatness as the Ash'aris have said, and not in the form of seizing as the Mu'tazilah said. He descends every night to the lower heaven, as He pleases; not only His mercy and reward [descend], as the Mu'tazilah and Ash'aris claimed. He is separate from His creations, no place is removed from His knowledge, and it is impermissible to describe Him as being everywhere. Rather, it must be said that He is in the heaven, above the Throne, as he (Exalted in His praise) has said, "The Most Merciful [who is] above the Throne established." [Ṭâhâ 20:5], and He said, "To Him ascends good speech, and righteous work raises it." [Fâṭir 35:10] ... Ahmad ibn Ḥanbal (rA) said shortly before his death, "The reports about the attributes should be passed as they came without *tashbeeh* (assimilation) or *ta'ṭeel* (negation)" ... We read the verse and report and we believe in what is in them, and we consign the modality of the attributes to the knowledge of Allah (Exalted is He), as Sufyân ibn 'Uyaynah said, "As Allah has described Himself in His Book; its explanation is its recitation, [there is] no other explanation." And we do not pursue other than that, for it is *ghayb*, and there is no place for reason in apprehending it. We ask Allah for forgiveness and safety and seek refuge in Him from saying about Him and His attributes what He and His Messenger have not informed us of.[49]

Imam Ibn al-Qayyim (rA) says in the introduction to al-*Kâfiyah al-Shâfiyah*,

We say about these issues exactly what our Lord and our Prophet say. We describe God using the

---

[49] 'Abd al-Qâdir al-Jeelâni, *al-Ghunyah*, 2nd ed., ed. Salâḥ ibn Muhammad ibn 'Uwaydah (Beirut: Dâr al-Kutub al-'Ilmiyyah, 1417/1997), 1:123-125.

words He uses to describe Himself and the words His Prophet used to describe God. We do not distort the text; we do not negate the divine attributes; we do not assimilate God to created beings; we do not find similarities between God and the created beings (*min ghayr taḥreef wa-lâ ta'ṭeel wa-min ghayr tashbeeh wa-lâ tamtheel*). We affirm the same names and attributes that God affirms for Himself. We negate the existence of any defect and flaw in Him. We negate any resemblance between Him and the created beings. Our approach is affirmation without assuming similarities between Him and the created beings, and de-anthropomorphism without negating the divine attributes (*ithbât bi-lâ tamtheel wa-tanzeeh bi-lâ ta'ṭeel*). Anyone who assimilates God to His creation is a heretic. Anyone who denies the attributes by which God describes Himself is a heretic. [Using] the attributes used by God and His Prophet to describe God is not anthropomorphism. The anthropomorphist worships an idol, and the negator of the divine attributes worships *'adam* (nothingness). However, the monotheist worships the one eternal God. "Nothing can be compared with Him. He alone hears all and sees all" (Q. 42:11).[50]-[xix]

---

[50] Ahmad ibn Ibrâheem Ibn 'Eesa, *Tawḍeeḥ al-Maqâṣid wa Taṣḥeeḥ al-*

Applying this to individual attributes, Imam al-Ṭabari (rA) said,

> We affirm all of those meanings that were mentioned in the scriptural reports of the Book and Revelation, as understood through literal affirmation, and we deny assimilation, so we say that He (Exalted is His praise) hears the sounds, not with an opening in the ear, and not with an organ like the children of Adam; likewise, He sees objects with a vision that is unlike the vision of the children of Adam, which is by their organs; He has two hands, and a right hand, and fingers, and they are not appendages, but His hands are outstretched with favors upon His creatures, not withholding; [He has] a face that is unlike the appendages of the creatures, which are made of flesh and blood; and we say that He laughs to whomever He pleases of His creations, and we do not say that this means the showing of teeth, and He descends to the lower heaven.[51]-[xx]

Qawâ'id fi Sharḥ Qaṣeedat ibn al-Qayyim al-Kâfiyah al-Shâfiyah, 3rd ed., ed. Zuhayr al-Shaweesh (Beirut: al-Maktab al-Islâmi, 1406H) 1:28. Translation adapted from Holtzman, "Accused of Anthropomorphism," 561-587.

[51] Muhammad ibn Jareer al-Ṭabari, *al-Tabṣeer fi Ma'âlim al-Deen*, ed. 'Ali ibn 'Abd al-'Azeez al-Shibl (Riyadh: Dâr al-'Âṣimah, 1416/1996), 142.

Our Tanzeeh

Tanzeeh means the exoneration of Allah from all deficiencies. It is the affirmation of His utter transcendence and incomparability. As affirmationists, we must place a special emphasis on *tanzeeh* because we are at greater risk of anthropomorphism than an absolute *mu'aṭṭil* (negationist), although it may also be said that *ta'ṭeel* is in itself a consequence of *tashbeeh*. Our affirmation of His transcendence and incomparability must thoroughly inform our discourse on the Divine attributes.

Before we teach the public about the attributes and our affirmation of the scriptural discourse on them at face value, we must start with a thick primer of *tanzeeh*, lest we lead them into a reprehensible conception of an anthropomorphic god. This is a natural tendency that requires effort to combat. Peter Westh adequately highlighted this tendency when he wrote,

> Once the mind has assigned a phenomenon to one of these ontological categories, it will automatically and unconsciously deliver up a host of tacit assumptions or "non-reflective beliefs" about it. The categories are hierarchically nested, so that intentional agents are usually understood to be living beings [of course! But what kind of life?] and living beings to be physical objects. [52]

Our *tanzeeh* has been rooted in the following.

God's incomparability and our incapacity to imagine Him or ascribe a modality to His attributes or know their ontological reality

□لَيْسَ كَمِثْلِهِ شَيْءٌ ۖ وَهُوَ السَّمِيعُ الْبَصِيرُ□

> "There is nothing like unto Him, and He is
> the Hearing, the Seeing." [Al-Shoorâ 42:11]

Yahya ibn 'Ammâr (rA) said,

> We do not need in this respect to say more than this: to believe in Him, and deny any modality of Him and beware of doubts, and be certain in that which Allah (glory be to Him) and His Messenger (pbuh) spoke of without reflecting [on its nature] or subjecting it to conjecture, impulses, or obsessions, and know with certainty that any modality, form, or similitude that crosses your mind, Allah is unlike it. We say he is above the Throne and His knowledge is everywhere.[53]-[xxi]

There is no problem, Imam Ibn 'Abd al-Barr (rA) maintains, in affirming a meaning without modality.[54][xxii]- Imam Ibn Taymiyyah (rA) argues that we cannot even

---

[52] Westh, "Anthropomorphism in God Concepts," 396–414.

[53] Abu al-Qâsim Ismail ibn Muhammad al-Aṣbahâni, *al-Ḥujjah fi Bayân al-Maḥajjah*, 2nd ed., ed. Muhammad ibn Rabee' al-Madkhali (Riyadh: Dâr al-Râyah, 1419/1999), 2:109.

[54] Ibn 'Abd al-Barr, *Al-Tamheed,* 7:137.

know the modality by which the spirit (*rooḥ*) is described in the Revelation as powerful, hearing, ascending, and descending, and he maintains that "if the spirit is qualified with these attributes, but without resemblance to those of the other created things, then the Creator is more deserving of His distinction from His creatures while being qualified with His names and attributes."[55]

Strict adherence to the text of Revelation with complete rejection of concomitants (*lawâzim*) that are not revealed

Some scholars, in reference to the hadith of Allah's descent to the lower heaven, have said that He descends in person (*bi-dhâtih*; with His ipseity); Nu'aym ibn Ḥammâd stated this, and even Ibn Taymiyyah mentioned it once.[56-xxiii] Ibn 'Abd al-Barr, on the other hand, while affirming the literal descent, rejected the addition of *bi-dhâtih* because it was not part of the statement of the Prophet (pbuh).[57-xxiv] Ibn 'Abd al-Barr's position on this matter is superior. Also, as it pertains to the descent of the Lord, some Atharis spoke of movement, including al-Dârimi (rA), but you find others objecting to this, like al-Khaṭṭâbi (rA).[58-xxv] Ibn al-Qayyim (rA), in following his teacher, favored a

[55] Ibn Taymiyyah, *Majmoo' al-Fatâwa*, 3:33.

[56] Ibn Taymiyyah, *Majmoo' al-Fatâwa*, 5:373.

[57] Ibn 'Abd al-Barr, *Al-Tamheed*, 7:144-145.

[58] Abu Sulaymân Ḥamd ibn Muhamma al-Khaṭṭâbi, *Ma'âlim al-Sunan* (Aleppo: al-Maṭba'ah al-'Ilmiyyah, 1351/1932), 4:332.

suspension of judgment regarding terms that have not been revealed, such as movement, relocation, corpus, direction, spatial locatedness, composition, and change.[59-xxvi] Imam Ibn Taymiyyah (rA) found the interpolation of those terminologies and discursive techniques in the theological discussions an innovation, condemning the use of terms like body, substance, direction, or supervening of originated events in the Divine essence while speaking about God.[60-xxvii] Based on this amodal affirmation, when it comes to the hadith of Allah's descent, we would have no obligation to entertain the objection of the third portion of the night varying for different people in different parts of the planet, because it is based on the questioner's *tashbeeh* of God to His creations and understanding His descent to be similar to ours, creating this difficulty for them.

Some Atharis described Allah as having a *ḥadd* (spatial extent), such as the great Imam Ibn al-Mubârak,[61-xxviii] al-Dârimi,[62-xxix] and others. Imam Ibn Taymiyyah tried to

---

[59] Shams al-Deen Muhammad ibn Abi Bakr Ibn Qayyim al-Jawziyyah, *Mukhtaṣar al-Ṣawâ'iq al-Mursalah 'alâ al-Jahmiyyah wa al-Mu'aṭṭilah*, abbr. Ibn al-Muṣili Muhammad ibn 'Abd al-Kareem al-Ba'li (Cairo: Dâr al-Ḥadeeth, 1422/2001), 472.

[60] Ibn Taymiyyah, *Dar' Ta'âruḍ al-'Aql wa al-Naql*, 1:239.

[61] al-Dârimi, *Naqḍ al-Imâm Abi Sa'eed al-Dârimi 'ala al-Ma'eesi*, ed. Rasheed ibn Ḥassan al-Alma'i (Riyadh: Maktabat al-Rushd, 1418/1998), 1:224.

[62] Dârimi, *Naqḍ al-Imâm Abi Sa'eed al-Dârimi 'ala al-Ma'eesi*, 1:223.

reconcile between their position and the position of those who rejected such description by saying that those who spoke of a spatial extent only meant that He is separate from his creation, not subsisting in them. It is always safer, though, to limit ourselves to the scriptural wording.

When it is said that Allah's aboveness means directionality, and that means corporealism, (which according to Ibn Rushd was not a rational *lâzim* [concomitant]),[63-xxx] we must reject any such *lawâzim*. We must not agree to anything that is not of the revealed description. All those concomitants and inferences are simply a function of the human categories of thought that are limited by our worldly experience of the *shahâdah* (seen). The *ghayb* (unseen) is unlike any of that, and Allah, in particular, is unlike anything else, and thus cannot be subject to our limited categories of thought.[64-xxxi]

Rejection of the *ẓâhir* that comes to the minds of anthropomorphists

Without a foundation of *tanzeeh* that instills in us Allah's incomparability, some of the audience may liken the attributes of Allah to those of His creations. Some may even say that this is what comes to mind first when they hear 'hand,' 'face,' 'coming,' and the like. The answer to this is that the one who used those terms is the one who

---

[63] Ibn Taymiyyah, *Dar' Ta'âruḍ al-'Aql wa al-Naql*, 6:214.

[64] Ibn 'Abd al-Barr, *Al-Tamheed*, 7:135.

said, "...nothing like unto Him." As Imam Ibn Katheer (rA) said, "the apparent implication that comes first to the minds of anthropomorphists is rejected."[65-xxxii] So when one asks if we believe in the attributes literally, we should first ask them what they mean by "literally"! The linguistic *ẓawâhir* (apparent meanings) are not limited to the imagination of a certain subset of people. After all, as Imam Ibn 'Abd al-Barr said,[66-xxxiii] we believe that death comes to us in truth (*ḥaqeeqah*) without all the concomitants of *tanaqqul* (changing places) they ascribe to the primary meanings of the following verse:

﴿وَجَاءَ رَبُّكَ وَالْمَلَكُ صَفًّا صَفًّا﴾

> "And your Lord has come and the angels,
> rank upon rank." [Al-Fajr 89:22]

A nominalist approach to language

Nominalism is the view that there are no universals in the extramental reality, that universals exist only in the mind, and in reality, only particular things exist. This is in contrast with Platonic realism that presumed ontological existence of universals, like redness, cat-ness, man-ness, hand-ness, face-ness, for example, as extant mind-independent abstract patterns of which particular objects

---

[65] Ibn Katheer, Tafseer al-Quran al-'Aẓeem, 3:383. Abu al-Fidâ' Ismail ibn Umar. *Tafseer al-Quran al-'Aẓeem.* Edited by Muhammad Ḥusayn Shams al-Deen. Beirut: Dâr al-Kutub al-'Ilmiyyah, 1419H.

[66] Ibn 'Abd al-Barr, *Al-Tamheed,* 7:137.

are copies in which these forms are inherent. In order for God and humans to share the same qualities by the mere virtue of being described by the same names, such qualities must have an existence in reality in which they participate. This is not true. Imam Ibn Taymiyyah (rA), who spoke of nominalism before William of Ockham[67] and other European nominalists did, stressed the fact that only particular things exist in reality. He argued, for instance, that the revealed sources describe numerous things in Paradise such as foods, clothes, marriage, and so on, but Ibn 'Abbâs said, "There is nothing in Paradise that is of this world except the names." If that may be said about the incomparability of creations among themselves, what may be said about the incomparability of God to His creations? Once the attribute is particularized to a certain being, its meaning is commensurate with its essence. The knowledge of God is not in any way like our knowledge. It is eternal, necessary, and all-inclusive.

Philosophy is much more flexible now than the peripatetic philosophy of the Middle Ages that Muslim philosophers, the Mu'tazilah, and the Mutakallimoon had to contend with. However, no matter how much you concede to "standard" philosophical principles, you will not be consistent unless you truly make them the measuring rod and reinterpret the Revelation to strictly

---

[67] William of Ockham (d. 1347 CE) was an English Franciscan (monk) philosopher who espoused metaphysical nominalism.

accord with them. This was something not even the Mu'tazilah could countenance, let alone the Mutakallimoon. The result is inconsistency in either case.

Nominalism was Ibn Taymiyyah's way of shifting the paradigm and cleverly formulating the concept that Ibn Rushd had expressed about the one truth and two languages, or what Wittgenstein would later call two "language games." However, Ibn Taymiyyah achieved this without detracting from the epistemic value of the declarative part of the Revelation. His common degree (*al-qadr al-mushtarak*) theory was to affirm the coherence of the scriptural language and its comprehensibility. We can confidently say that the Taymiyyan project with respect to the qualities of the Divine was to transfer the discussion from the philosophy of metaphysics to the philosophy of language.

The style of presentation and its effect on the audience

The way of teaching the names and attributes of the Divine to the public should take into consideration that many people incline toward anthropomorphism and tend to infer from the seen about the unseen. It is for this reason that mentioning, one after another, all those attributes that may lead to this conception of God, must be avoided. It is not becoming of an imam in his Friday sermon to say that Allah has a face, eyes, hands, fingers, a leg (or shin), and He laughs, etc., and that is to avoid the resulting inappropriate cognitive synthesis.

While answering the Christians who accused Muslims of anthropomorphism, Imam Ibn Taymiyyah (rA) said,

> What you have mentioned about Muslims is a clear fabrication against them. This composition they mentioned is not in the Quran, nor is it in the Hadith; or has it been known that one of the Muslim scholars or a famous Muslim sect has spoken in the way they ascribed to them, when they claim that Muslims say that Allah has eyes with which he sees, hands that He stretches out, a leg (shin), and a face that He turns in all directions, and a side? However, those [people] have inappropriately and erroneously composed out of the statements of the Quran a composition, and have claimed that the Muslims speak in this manner.[68-xxxiv]

He also cited verses of the Bible that speak in the same way as the Quran of a "personal God" and other verses that can be seen as more anthropomorphic.

---

[68] Taqi al-Deen Ahmad ibn 'Abd al-Ḥaleem Ibn Taymiyyah, *al-Jawâb al-Ṣaḥeeḥ li man Baddala Deen al-Maseeḥ*, 2nd ed., eds. Ali ibn Hassan, 'Abd al-'Azeez ibn Ibrâheem, and Ḥamdân ibn Muhammad (Riyadh: Dâr al-'Âṣimah, 1419/1999), 4:411.

Our Affirmation

Our *tanzeeh* must be balanced by our acknowledgment of the integrity of the Revelation and our belief in the ultimate epistemic value of its declarative content. We believe that God described Himself to us in the Quran and through His Messenger in the Sunnah. We believe that He used the most suitable terms and descriptions to teach us about Him. Naturally, these descriptions had to be worded using human linguistic conventions and categories of understanding in order to be conceivable by our minds. God warned us, however, that we should not liken him to His creations or imagine a modality of His attributes beyond what He has told us. The Revelation used the most appropriate expressions to point to realities the true essence of which cannot be apprehended by the human minds. It is inconceivable to consign their meanings themselves to God. This would mean that He and His Messenger spoke to us in undecipherable language. It would require us to drop certain sentences and phrases from passages in the Quran and the Sunnah that are completely harmonious with the primary meanings of those sentences and phrases.

What Are the Ẓawâhir We Believe In?

The great Mâliki scholar al-Dardeer (rA) says in his commentary on his *Khareedah* that "mercy is the softness of the heart, and that is impossible with regard to Allah, so what is intended is being willing to favor and show kindness."[69] However, this also leads us to another problem, because "to will" is to have *gharaḍ* (interest) in the primary linguistic usage, according to the *Mutakallimeen*; whereas, also according to them, Allah is above that. Still, Imam al-Ghazâli said that the Revelation allowed the use of *irâdah* (will) in reference to Allah.[70] The Atharis may add that it also allowed the use of *raḥmah* (mercy). Likewise, the Ash'aris reinterpreted "to love" to mean 'to be pleased.' The Atharis affirm that Allah loves and is merciful, with mercy being an attribute of His. In fact, Imam al-Ṭabari (rA) argued that it is impossible that one shows mercy without having mercy.[71-xxxv] The difference is that the Atharis did not limit themselves to the lexical definitions of mercy, love, or will. There is no reason to think that the mercy of God or His love are not *haqeeqah* (literal). The lexicons were authored after the time of the first audience of the Revelation. We aim to understand the Quran through the linguistic conventions of their time. They never questioned the use of "mercy" or

---

[69] Ahmad ibn Ahmad al-Dardeer, *Sharḥ al-Khareedah al-Bâhiyyah*, ed. 'Abd al-Salâm ibn 'Abd al-Hâdi (Istanbul: Dâr al-Bayrooti, 2015), 16.

[70] See Abu Ḥâmid Muhammad ibn Muhammad al-Ghazâli, *Tahâfut al-Falâsifah*, 6th ed., ed. Sulaymân Dunya (Cairo: Dâr al-Ma'ârif, n.d.),103-104.

[71] al-Ṭabari, *al-Tabṣeer fi Ma'âlim al-Deen*, 141.

"love" with respect to God. If someone says that anger is "the boiling of the blood of the heart," making it unbefitting of God, we simply say that we do not believe that about God. We believe in His anger, as He spoke of it, but we do not believe that anger must mean "the boiling of the blood of the heart."

Our understanding of the *ẓawâhir* (apparent or primary meanings) of the Revelation depends, in addition to the conventions of the language, on two important hermeneutical principles: intertextuality and contextuality. So, when it comes to the interpretation of the verses that mention His presence with us wherever we are, we must reconcile them with the countless verses, hadiths, as well as rational proofs on Allah's transcendence and aboveness. Imam Ibn 'Abd al-Barr (rA) said, "...the scholars among the Companions and [their] Successors (*tâbi'een*), from whom knowledge of (interpretation of scripture) is taken, said, concerning the interpretation of this verse, that 'God is upon His Throne' and that 'His knowledge is in all places,' and no one whose opinion is considered authoritative has opposed them in this."[72]-[xxxvi] We do not even need to resort to reinterpretation. His *ma'iyyah* (with-ness) is real, and it is understood to mean that He is with us via his care, sight, hearing, knowledge, support, control, and power.

---

[72] Ibn 'Abd al-Barr, *Al-Tamheed,* 7:139.

Context is of paramount importance as well. There are no inherent meanings attached to words in the abstract. Words acquire meaning only in a contextualized usage. Take for example the hadith that says, "The Black Stone is God's right hand on Earth; whosoever shakes hands with it and kisses it, it is as if he had shaken hands with and kissed the right hand of God." Imam Ibn Taymiyyah (rA) said that the hadith is not an established authentic report, but that if it were authentic (which it is according to many scholars), then it would not need reinterpretation (*ta'weel*) because no one would understand from that context that the Black Stone is part of God or an attribute of His. The two indicants of this in the hadith, according to him, are: "on Earth" and "as if."[73]-[xxxvii]

Ibn al-Fâ'oos al-Ḥanbali (rA) said this hadith is *ḥaqeeqah* (literal), so Ibn al-Khâdibah (rA) used to call him "*al-ḥajari*" (the stone-man). We believe they (may Allah have mercy on them) were both wrong. We do not presume of a Muslim scholar that he meant that part of God is in fact that stone. Imam Ibn Rajab (rA) explained what he could have meant:

> Those of the scholars who denied metaphors would do this so that people would not ascribe this false meaning [that it has no implication], thus becoming

---

[73] Ibn Taymiyyah, *Dar' Ta'âruḍ al-'Aql wa al-Naql*, 3:384.

> a means to distorting the truths of the Quran and the Sunnah. They argued that most people who speak of "literal" and "allegorical" are the Mu'tazilah and their likes of the innovators, and they found a way through this to altering the speech after it was established. They would ban calling anything allegorical and make all speech literal. They say that when a word denotes something by itself, it is literal concerning this meaning, and when it denotes another meaning via a *qareenah* (secondary indicant), it is also literal concerning this other meaning... So, the word "right hand" in the hadith of "the heavens and earth are rolled up in His right hand" is literal and it refers to the attribute of the Divine ipseity, and in the hadith of the Black Stone, it is also literal, but it refers to that which is to be touched and kissed.[74]-[xxxviii]

Al-Dhahabi laments the unfortunate story and says, "It is, however, preferable to avoid involvement in [the debate regarding] literal or allegorical, for we have no need to qualify what was left unqualified by the *salaf*; but we should instead believe and stay silent. Our statement regarding this: literal versus allegorical is a form of ignorance and ineloquence."[75]-[xxxix]

---

[74] Zayn al-Deen 'Abd al-Rahman Ibn Rajab, *Rawâi' al-Tafseer: al-Jâmi' li Tafseer al-Imâm Ibn Rajab al-Ḥanbali*, ed. Abu Mu'âdh Ṭâriq ibn 'Awaḍ Allâh (Riyadh: Dâr al-'Âṣimah, 1422/2001), 2:255.

When the Companions heard the Prophet (pbuh) speaking about the angels sitting the deceased up in their graves after their burial, they never questioned the modality of that or said, "How?" When he (pbuh) told them that the sun (which the Quran describes as a lamp floating around an orbit) prostrates at sunset before God, they never questioned the modality of that or said it was allegorical or tried to give it a different meaning. This is despite these things being to a great extent of the world of *shahâdah* (seen). They got the intended message and did not argue about hyper-technicalities.

But we do believe that there are certain matters that God chose to tell us about in these terms because they were most suitable to denote them in our human languages and according to our human categories of thought. He chose *yuḥibb* (loves) to tell us of His, well, 'love' of the pious. He could have chosen any other word such as *riḍâ* (pleasure) or *qabool* (acceptance), but He chose *ḥubb* (love). Now, any implications of deficiency associated with human love are not to be ascribed to Him of course. Nothing is like Him, and none of the qualities of His creations are like His, so His love is unlike any love we experience. The obvious meanings that we believe in are those which are apprehended from the text and linguistic

---

[75] al-Dhahabi, *Siyar A'lâm al-Nubalâ'*, 14:368.

conventions, by minds primed with the transcendence and incomparability of God.

What Is the Common Degree/Overlap (*al-Qadr al-Mushtarak*)?

When we say that Allah is existent and we are existent, or that He is hearing and we are hearing, or that he is merciful, and then he describes His Messenger as merciful, what does that mean? Are these words as they apply to God and others simply homonyms sharing the same letters and having completely different meanings? Or is there a common degree, a meaning in common between them, or a connotational overlap? If we say the first, then why are their primary meanings always harmonious with the context? And why would Allah use them in the first place to tell us about Himself, if they would not imply anything to us? But if we say that there *is* a common meaning, how is that not likening or assimilating God to His creations?

To answer this, Imam Ibn Taymiyyah (rA) argues that the common degree is only a conceptual notion in the mind, not an ontological reality. If we do not know what hearing is, we would never understand what Allah means by calling Himself *al-Samee'* (the all-hearing). The same applies to the other attributes. However, that commonality has no extramental reality, so the *ishtirâk* (participation) is only in the mind, but when the words are applied to particular entities in the reality, there is no commonality or similarity, because it will apply to each entity commensurate with that entity's ipseity. Therefore, while our understanding of the word 'knowledge' helps us understand what is meant by the verses and hadiths that speak of Allah's knowledge, there is no similarity at all between our originated, contingent, limited knowledge and His pre-eternal, necessary, all-inclusive knowledge.[76]-[xl]

The fact that Allah uses comparative and superlative adjectives (such as greater, better, higher, etc.) in the Quran to describe Himself, and that the Prophet (pbuh) uses them in the Sunnah, is sufficient to prove that there is a degree of notional commonality of connotations that does not indicate assimilation.

[76] Ibn Taymiyyah, *Majmoo' al-Fatâwa*, 5:346.

WHY DO WE BELIEVE IN AMODAL AFFIRMATION AND WHY DO WE BELIEVE IT IS IMPORTANT?

Because the *Ẓâhir* Is What Should Be Believed Until Proven Otherwise

The danger of diverting the significance of the revealed text from their primary meanings to secondary or esoteric ones does not need to be emphasized. Nations before us were condemned by God because of doing this. Allah says,

﴿يُحَرِّفُونَ الْكَلِمَ مِن بَعْدِ مَوَاضِعِهِ﴾

“They distort words beyond their [proper] usages.” [Al-Mâ'idah 5:41]

Some Muslim scholars claimed that this was the only type of distortion of the previous scriptures. They denied that the words themselves were altered, but only their meanings. While we do not believe in that proposition, we do not belittle the gravity of distorting the meanings even while retaining the letter of the text. This is why Imam Ibn

'Abd al-Barr (rA) says, after he rebuts the reinterpretation of *istiwâ'*,

> It is the right of the text to be understood in accordance with its primary meaning until the Ummah agrees that an allegorical meaning was intended. This is because there is no other way to properly follow what has been sent down to us from our Lord. The speech of Allah should be understood to mean its more common and obvious implications unless there is a compelling hindrance precluding that. If it is excusable to claim allegory by any claimant, no statement will survive. Allah is exalted above speaking except in a language comprehensible by the Arabs according to their linguistic conventions.[77]-[xli]

Factors that would preclude the primary meaning would include consensus of Muslim scholars, as Ibn 'Abd al-Barr says, as well as an irreconcilable conflict with another definitive text of Revelation or the deliverances of empirical senses or *badeehi* reason, which must be validated by human concurrence, as we indicated in the discussion about epistemology. As we have seen, and as we will further discuss, we do not find the *ẓawâhir* of the scriptural reports about the attributes to be in intractable conflict with any of these factors. In fact, it is not only

[77] Ibn 'Abd al-Barr, *Al-Tamheed,* 7:131.

Atharis who believe in that. As mentioned in our discussion earlier on conflict between reason and Revelation, Imam al-Taftazâni (rA) stated,

> If it is said, if the correct religious belief is the negation of spatial locatedness and directionality, why is it then that the heavenly scriptures and the Prophetic traditions imply in countless instances the affirmation of that without a single instance of negating it? The answer is: because exoneration from directionality is something the intellects of the masses cannot comprehend, to the extent that they would be certain that something that does not exist in any direction does not exist at all. [Therefore,] a discourse with apparent assimilation (*tashbeeh*) was more suitable in addressing them and calling them to the religion and more conducive to their uprightness.[78]- [xlii]

Most Atharis do not speak of directionality, but rather of *'uluw* (aboveness), and it is hard to believe that God would lead the masses to what the Mutakallimoon describe as disbelief; nevertheless, the observation of Imam al-Taftazâni (rA) about the abundance of textual reports affirming the attributes in question and the lack of any to counter that affirmation is wholly accurate.

---

[78] al-Taftazâni, *Sharḥ al-Maqâṣid*, 3:36.

Because the Revelation Should Be Hermeneutically Self-Sufficient

The use of *kalâm* in defense of our established creed is commendable. However, this is only so as long as it is invoked after we establish the creedal principles from the Revelation, in accordance with the linguistic conventions of the first community and their expressed understanding. Within this context we understand Imam Ahmad's critique of the great ascetic and scholar al-Hârith al-Muḥâsibi's engagement with the philosophical discourse. Ahmad (rA) feared that this well-intended engagement in defense of Islamic doctrines may eventually have untoward side effects. We have an established interpretation methodology in our legal theory that enables us to understand the text of Revelation. Our legal theory also respected the office of reason and placed a lot of weight on the concepts of intertextuality and contextuality. Subjecting the process of deduction to a foreign discourse and its principles creates inconsistency and tension within the process. For instance, the Aristotelian principle that the Divine and His radical simplicity preclude His qualification by any attributes is a xenograft[79] that cannot be transplanted into our legal theory without a major chaotic reaction.

---

[79] In medicine, a xenograft is a tissue graft or organ transplant from a donor of a different species from the recipient. Such a procedure may end up harming the recipient.

In addition to pointing out the erroneousness of inferring from the *shahâdah* (seen) about the *ghayb* (unseen), using amodalism and nominalism should be our defenses against the charges of the philosophers. Otherwise, we will be at best inconsistent, and at worst, forced into a full retreat to negative theology and complete agnosticism.

Because This Is What the First Community Believed In

It has been reported from Umm Salamah (rAa), Rabee'ah (rA), and Mâlik (rA) that they said,

"الاِسْتِوَاءُ غَيْرُ مَجْهُولٍ وَالْكَيْفُ غَيْرُ مَعْقُولٍ"

> "God's settling [on the Throne] is not unknown, but the modality of it is not apprehensible."

There are variations of this report from Mâlik, with the one above reported by al-Bayhaqi being the strongest. However, there is no substantive difference between the different narrations, whether he said that *istiwâ'* was "known" or "not unknown," or the modality "unknown" or "not apprehensible," the message is clear. The meaning of the word is known, but the modality, ultimate essence, or ontological reality of this meaning is unknown. (The matter of consigning meaning/modality to God is discussed later on.)

Imam al-Tirmidhi (rA) said, concerning one of the hadiths he reported about Allah's right hand:

> This is how it has been reported from Mâlik, Sufyan ibn `Uyaynah, and `Abd Allâh ibn al-Mubârak, that

they said about these narrations, "Pass them on without [ascribing] a modality." This is the statement of the people of knowledge of Ahl al-Sunnah wa al-Jamâ'ah. As for the Jahmiyyah, they rejected these narrations and said that this is *tashbeeh.* In more than one place in the Qur'an, Allah Mentioned His *yad* (hand), *baṣar* (sight) and *sam`* (hearing); The Jahmiyyah reinterpreted these verses and explained them differently from the way the people of knowledge explained them, and said: "Allah did not create Adam with His Hand." They said, "The meaning of *yad* (hand) here is 'power' (*quwwah*)." Isḥâq ibn Ibrâheem said, "*Tashbeeh* is when one says: hand like my hand, or similar to my hand, or hearing like my hearing, or similar to my hearing, then this is *tashbeeh.* But if one says what Allah has said: 'hand,' 'hearing,' 'seeing,' and does not speak of modality, nor does he say, 'like my hearing,' then it is not *tashbeeh.*' It is what Allah, the Most Blessed and Most High, said in His Book: 'There is none like Unto Him, and he is the all-Hearing, the all-Seeing'."[80]-[xliii]

Imam Abu Ḥanifah (rA) said,

---

[80] Abu 'Eesa, Muhammad ibn 'Eesa al-Tirmidhi, *Sunan al-Tirmidhi*, ed. Bashshâr 'Awwâd Ma'roof (Beirut: Dâr al-Gharb al-Islâmi, 1998), 2:43.

> He has a hand, a face, and a self, as Allah the Exalted mentioned in the Quran, so whatever Allah the Exalted mentioned in the Quran of the face, hand, and self is an attribute of His without a modality. It should not be said that His hand is His power or His favor, for that would involve negation of the attribute.[81]-[xliv]

Imam Abu al-Ḥasan al-Ash'ari said,

> Ahl al-Sunnah and the Hadith scholars said: He is not a body and He is not similar to anything, and He is above the Throne, as He (Exalted is He) has said, "The Most Merciful [who is] above the Throne, established." We do not oppose Allah in His statements, but we say that He established Himself above the Throne, without (ascribing any) modality.[82]-[xlv]

Because, to Us, the Alternatives of *Ta'weel* and *Tafweeḍ* of Meaning Are Not Valid

While Imam al-Juwayni (rA) never refuted *ta'weel* or *tafweeḍ* in favor of affirmation, he did refute them each at

---

[81] al-Nu'mân ibn Thâbit Abu Ḥanifah, *al-Fiqh al-Akbar* (UAE: Maktabat al-Furqân, 1419/1999), 27.

[82] Abu al-Ḥassan 'Ali ibn Ismâ'eel al-Ash'ari, *Maqâlât al-Islâmiyeen*, 3rd ed., ed. Hellmut Ritter (Wiesbaden: Franz Steiner, 1400/1980), 211.

different times in favor of the other, and both of his refutations were accurate. He first said about *tafweeḍ*,

> Avoiding *ta'weel* out of fear from falling into error in belief brings about confusion and ambiguity and pushes the public into error, and leads to misconceptions concerning the foundations of the religion, and subjects the Book of Allah to conjecture.[83]-[xlvi]

Later in his life, he condemned *ta'weel* as an innovation that the predecessors strictly avoided. He said,

> The imams of the predecessors refrained from *ta'weel*, leaving the explicit wording of the texts to stand as is and consigning their true meaning to the Lord Most High. The opinion we accept and adopt in religious matters is to follow the *salaf* of the Ummah, as it is preferable to follow them and to refrain from innovation. The definitive scriptural evidence in this respect is that the consensus of the Ummah is a proof, and it is the greatest authority in the Sharia. The Companions of the Messenger of Allah (pbuh) have consistently avoided engaging their meanings and [endeavoring to] comprehend what is in them, and they are the elites of Islam who were always concerned with the duties of Sharia, and they saved no effort in laying out the principles

---

[83] Al-Juwayni, *al-Irshâd* (Sa'âdah), 42.

> of the religion, encouraging one another to preserve it, teaching the people what they needed. Had reinterpretation of these primary meanings been excusable or necessary, their occupation with it would have been greater than their occupation with the details of practice. So, if their generation and that of the *tâbi'een* ended while they were refraining from *ta'weel*, then that would be a definitive proof that it is the view to be followed.[84]-[xlvii]

Which *ta'weel* did the imam say was rejected by the early predecessors? Well, *ta'weel* has three meanings:

1. The very ontological reality of a matter and its very essence or outcome;
2. The *tafseer* (explanation) of its meaning; many of the earlier exegetes would call *tafseer ta'weel*; and
3. The deflection of the primary (*ẓâhir*) meaning in favor of a secondary (*majâzi*) one.

The first meaning of *ta'weel* belongs to Allah alone, particularly concerning the knowledge of the unseen. The second belongs to all people who speak the language of the Revelation, concerning its clear statements, and to the scholars well-grounded in knowledge, concerning its intricate ones. The third is the subject of this controversy. I have quoted in the previous discussions many proofs against *ta'weel* in this third sense. It is at least largely

---

[84] al-Juwayni, *Al-'Aqeedah al-Nizâmiyyah*, 31.

agreed upon that the righteous predecessors did not engage in it. In the next segment, we will discuss whether they consigned the meanings of the verses, or only their modality and ultimate ontological reality, to the knowledge of God.

Here is a detailed answer rejecting *ta'weel* of the hands of Allah as his power or favor, from the great imam of the early Ash'aris, al-Bâqillâni (rA):

> If they said, "Why do you deny that what is meant by His statement 'whom I created with My two hands' [could be] that he created him with His power or favor? Because 'the hand' in the language could mean 'favor' or 'power,' as it may be said, 'So-and-so owes me a white hand,' meaning a favor, and it may be said, 'This matter is in so-and-so's hand, or under his hand,' meaning that it is under his control or ownership. It is also said, 'a man who is *ayd* (pl. of *yad*),' if he is capable... Likewise, His saying 'whom I created with My two hands' means 'with my power and favor'." It would be said to them [in response], "This is false, because His saying 'with My two hands' indicates the affirmation of two hands which are an attribute of His. If what is intended is [His] power, then He must then have two powers, and you do not even affirm one power for the Creator (Exalted is He), so how can you ascribe to Him two? The Muslims, both

affirmationists and negationists, have also unanimously agreed that it is impossible that Allah has two powers, so what you have said is proven false. It is also not possible that Allah had created Adam with two favors because the favors of Allah upon Adam and others cannot be counted..." What further proves the falsity of what they said is that, if it is true, Iblees would have not missed it, and would have said, "What virtue does Adam then have over me requiring that I prostrate to him? I, too, was created by Your hand, which is Your power and favor"... If it is said, "Why, then, would you deny that His face and hand are appendages, since you do not apprehend [in the reality around you] a face or a hand that is not an appendage?," it would be said [in response], "That is not necessary, and it is not necessary since we and you do not apprehend a living, capable, knowing being except that it is a *jism* (corpus, body), that we [should] ascribe that to Allah, nor is it necessary for one who is self-subsistent to be a substance or a corpus just because we and you do not find anyone who is not like that in our witnessed experience."[85]-[xlviii]

---

[85] Abu Bakr Muhammad ibn al-Ṭayyib al-Bâqillâni, *Tamheed al-Awâ'il wa Talkheeṣ al-Dalâ'il*, ed. 'Imâd al-Deen Ahmad Ḥaydar (Beirut: Mu'assasat al-Kutub al-Thaqâfiyyah, 1407/1987), 295.

So, what do we mean by the 'hands' if we deny that they are parts or appendages? The mention of the hands indicates agency and may be used to refer to generosity or favor in one context, power or domination in another, and support and allegiance in yet another. The hand also refers to affability, as in 'handshaking.' The Exalted chose to use those expressions of "hand," "hands," "two hands," and "right hand," so instead of the conundrum of *ta'weel*, we can just deny assimilations, resemblances, modalities, and conceiving of hands that are parts or appendages, and let the message reach the audience unimpeded, with the full strength and richness of the rhetorical style of the Revelation.

Imam al-Juwayni (rA) did not see a difference between the attributes the early Ash'aris reinterpreted, such as those about 'descent' and 'coming,' and those they affirmed, such as the 'hands,' 'face,' and 'eyes.'[86]-[xlix] The pretext of reinterpreting the first group, which involves the claimed impossibility of succession of originated events in the Divine ipseity, is different from reinterpreting the second, which is likening God to His creations. Nonetheless, we agree with the imam (rA) that they are ultimately the same in the sense that their affirmation is rooted in the same hermeneutical principles. No philosophical principle may compel us to deny the primary implications of the scriptures, because our

---

[86] al-Juwayni, *al-Irshâd* (Sa'âdah), 138.

understanding of it is flexible enough and humble enough to preclude an intractable conflict with reason.

Now, the second question is, did the predecessors in fact consign the meanings to God, as claimed by some of the imams among the *Mutakallimeen*?

In addition to the reason mentioned by Imam al-Juwayni for the rejection of *tafweeḍ*, our denial of this is based on its near impossibility. If the predecessors truly rejected the primary meanings, they would have been much clearer about it, so as to warn people about them. To say that the meaning is unknown is to say that God has spoken to us in countless places in His Book and through His Messenger in undecipherable language, contrary to what He has told us. This would also mean that when the Prophet (pbuh) was teaching the Companions about these matters, he did not know what he was teaching, and they did not know what they were hearing. Additionally, it would mean that we have to ignore whole sentences or even paragraphs while reading the Quran or Sunnah and treat them as disjointed letters. All this is when their primary meanings are in complete harmony with the surrounding text. What are we to make of the Prophet's statement, "Allah laughs for two men who kill each other and end up in paradise?" In fact, we cannot even translate '*yaḍḥak*' into 'laugh,' nor can we translate all those reports, because their meanings are unknown.

What did they consign to God then? The understanding of the attributes is based on two principles, flexibility and humbleness: the flexible understanding of the denotational role of languages rooted in nominalism or conceptual nominalism, and our humbleness in recognizing that the language of the Revelation simply points out to us concepts whose ontological reality is completely beyond our apprehension. The predecessors used both principles to accept the primary meanings of the reports with submission and to relegate their ultimate ontological reality, modality, and "how-ness" to God Most High.

Here is what Ibn 'Arabi (rA),[87] a most revered figure in many circles of organized *taṣawwuf*, says about *tafweeḍ*:

[87] A number of our greatest scholars excommunicated or hereticated Ibn 'Arabi for statements and writings that cannot be excused as *shaṭaḥât* (esoteric utterances made during spiritual trances). They include al-'Izz Ibn Abd al-Salâm, Ibn Taymiyyah, al-Subki, al-Bulqeeni, al-Biqâ'i, Ibn Hajar, and many others. While this writer does not fault those scholars, he finds it safer for us now to avoid excommunication and simply warn all non-discerning beginners about his written legacy. We must declare the statements of *kufr* as such. However, the knowledge on which these scholars based their excommunication fatwas may have been certain to them, but it reached us confounded with possibilities (although remote) of alternative interpretations of his statements or that they were interpolations against him. There is also the possibility that he repented and recanted those statements. I find the position of Imam al-'Irâqi to be safer for us, which is that "his books contained explicit statements of *kufr*." *Taqleed* is done out of necessity, and there is no necessity in

> One group said, "We believe in this wording as it came, without comprehending its meaning, until we become in this belief like one who did not hear [it], and we hold on to the indicants of reason that precluded the primary meaning of this statement." This group is also stubborn, but uses refined rhetoric, and they rejected what came to them from Allah with that rhetoric. They made themselves like those who had not heard this [Divine] speech. Another group said, "We believe in the wording according to what Allah knows about it and [what] His Messenger [knows about it]." Those said [in effect] that Allah spoke to us in vain because He addressed us with that which we do not comprehend, whereas [on the contrary] Allah says, "And We did not send any messenger except [speaking] in the language of his people to state clearly for them." [Ibrâheem 14:4] He (pbuh) brought this, and he made it clear as Allah said, but those denied that it was clear.[88]-[1]

---

excommunicating someone who lived 800 hundred years ago. Having said that, it is known that he was a brilliant author, which made someone like Imam Ibn Taymiyyah initially hold him in high esteem. Those scholars who are well-grounded in knowledge may be able to extract benefits from his writings.

[88] Muḥyee al-Deen Muhammad ibn Ali Ibn 'Arabi, *Al-Futuḥât al-Makkiyyah* (Beirut: Dâr al-Kutub al-'Ilmiyyah, n.d.), 7:11.

There are statements that were reported from the *salaf* and the imams that are cited in support of *tafweeḍ al-ma'nâ* (consigning the meaning) to Allah. In some report from Ahmad related by Ḥanbal about the scriptural attributes, he reported that Ahmad said, "We believe in them and accept them without modality or meaning." It is known that Ḥanbal's solitary reports from the imam are controversial. However, if the authenticity of this is established, the negation of meaning must be understood, in light of the imam's strict affirmationism, to mean a denial of a meaning given to it other than the apparent. Anyone who reads al-Khallâl's reports of the imam's creed would not doubt that for a second.[89] After all, if Imam Ahmad used to consign meaning, there would have not been a disagreement between the Ḥanbalis and Ash'aris from the 4th century onward, unless it is suggested that the vast majority of Ḥanbalis did not understand the teachings of their imam.

Al-Waleed ibn Muslim said: "I asked al-Awza`i, al-Thawri, Mâlik ibn Anas, and al-Layth ibn Sa`d about the Hadeeths of *ṣifât* (attributes), and they replied, 'Pass them

---

[89] See for example Ahmad Ibn Ḥanbal, *al-'Aqeedah, Riwâyat Abi Bakr al-Khallâl*, ed. 'Abd al-'Azeez al-Sayrawan (Damascus: Dâr Qutaybah, 1408), 103-108.

on as they came, without [ascribing] modality'."[90]-[li] Sufyan Ibn `Uyaynah said, "Everything that Allah described Himself with in the Quran, its interpretation is its recitation, without modality" (al-Dâraqutni: "without modality or resemblance"; in some reports, "without explanation"). If this also established, it is explained by the reports that say "without modality." It may also mean 'without an explanation other than the obvious.'

While it is possible that some of them meant consigning the meaning to God, it is very unlikely, for the reasons mentioned above. In fact, these statements of the predecessors would mean that they only consigned the modality or ultimate nature of the attributes. Had they wanted to consign the meanings to God, they would have said, rather, "Let them pass while believing that what they indicate is not intended," or "Let them pass while believing that Allah is not to be described by what these words indicate." In such a case, they are not being passed the way they were relayed to us."[91]-[lii] Additionally, the very fact that they talked about consigning the *modality* or ultimate ontological reality to God means that they are not consigning the *meaning* to God, who addressed them with

---

[90] Ahmad ibn al-Ḥusayn al-Bayhaqi, *al-Sunan al-Kubra*, 3rd ed., ed. Muhammad 'Abd al-Qâdir 'Aṭa (Beirut: Dâr al-Kutub al-'Ilmiyyah, 1424/2003), 3:4.

[91] Ibn Taymiyyah, *Majmoo' al-Fatâwa*, 5:42.

this speech. Certainly, it would be senseless without establishing any meaning to speak of a modality: for what?

Moreover, the predecessors did explain what some of those verses and hadiths meant. Take for example the attribute of *istiwâ'*. Both Mujâhid, the imam of exegetes and student of Ibn 'Abbâs, and Abu al-'Âliyah, the famous narrator of the *tâbi'een*, interpreted this to mean "rose and ascended."[92]-[liii] Also, the explanation of certain verses with some of their implications is a known way of exegesis. So, when Allah speaks of the Prophet (pbuh) being *"bi a'yooninâ"* (in Our eyes), this of course means "in Our care and vision." This does not mean the negation of the attribute by someone who says so, unless that negation is expressed. When Allah speaks of the annihilation of all things except His face, of course we all understand that He means except Him. We do not conceive of the face as a part of the Divine in the first place, to be confused about the meaning of the verse.

Finally, it is possible that some of the *salaf* may have delegated the meanings, particularly if they had witnessed the whole controversy that took place after their era, and while it is hard to assume that all of them would have continued to have a unified detailed doctrine on these matters, it seems that there is no basis to claim that consigning the meaning (not just the ultimate ontological

---

[92] al-Bukhâri, *al-Jâmi' al-Ṣaḥeeḥ*, 9:124. Reported by him with an incomplete chain of transmission (isnâd) that was later completed.

reality) was the prevalent attitude of theirs, or would have been, had they lived long enough to witness the full-blown controversy.

Because It Is Important to Know God and Speak Correctly about Him

Allah says,

﴿وَلِلَّهِ الْأَسْمَاءُ الْحُسْنَىٰ فَادْعُوهُ بِهَا ۖ وَذَرُوا الَّذِينَ يُلْحِدُونَ فِي أَسْمَائِهِ ۚ سَيُجْزَوْنَ مَا كَانُوا يَعْمَلُونَ﴾

> "And to Allah belong the best names, so invoke Him by them. And leave [the company of] those who practice deviation concerning His names. They will be recompensed for what they have been doing." [Al-'A`râf 7:180]

There is nothing safer and farther from being deserving of the threat in this verse than describing God with that by which He described Himself and by which His Messenger described Him. The declarative part of the Sharia is not of less importance than its imperative part, which provides the moral–ethical framework. In fact, telling us about God is the most important and noblest aspect of the Revelation.

We repeat the supplication of Sulṭân al-Awliyâ', "We ask Allah for forgiveness and safety and seek refuge in Him from saying about Him and His attributes what He and His Messenger have not informed us of."[93]

Because the Epistemic Value of the Revelation Is at Stake

The claim of conflict between reason and the primary meanings of the Revelation leads to a cascade of departures from the Divine guidance. Fomenting such conflict in the minds of the masses may lead to unmeasurable and uncontrollable consequences. The undermining of the public's trust in the veracity and the supreme epistemic value of the Revelation is what is feared here. The rationalist theologians never agreed on what to accept and what to reject, to say that there could be clear lines. The pain and confusion that results from doubting the obvious implications of what we recite day and night is intolerable. After Imam al-Ghazâli (rA) discovered the futility of *kalâm*, he advocated for a much greater place for inspiration and mystic disclosure at the top of the epistemological pyramid. He described the way of Imam Ahmad as that which is limited to the purports of transmitted reports. He said,

> The middle path (*ḥadd al-iqtiṣâd*) between the "wantonness" (*inhilâl*) of excessive *ta'weel* [of the philosophers] and the "rigidity (*jumood*) of the Ḥanbalites" is a fine and subtle [line]

[93] al-Jeelâni, *al-Ghunyah,* 1:125.

> comprehensible only to those who have been granted success and who perceive things by a divine light, not by means of receiving transmitted knowledge (*samâʿ*). Then, when the hidden aspects of things are made manifest to them as they truly are, they consider the transmitted texts [of Revelation] and the wording thereof, and whatever agrees with what they have witnessed by the light of certainty, they affirm, and whatever disagrees with this, they reinterpret it.[94]-[liv]

While the importance of Divine assistance cannot be denied, there will be no standard to refer to in understanding the Divine message if it is not the obvious implications, as Imam Ibn ʻAbd al-Barr (rA) noted. Also, Imam Ibn Ḥazm (rA), a rationalist theologian himself, noted that there is no way to objectively choose someone's *ilhâm* (inspiration) over another's. The way of Imam Ahmad was the best defense against an esoteric interpretation of the text that may give some people, like the Bâṭiniyyah, the delusion that they may ignore the "outer" implications of the Revelation when they "contradict with reason" and develop hermeneutical systems that were foreign to the first community.

---

[94] al-Ghazâli, *Iḥyâ' ʻUloom al-Deen*, 1:104. Translation adapted from El-Tobgui, *Reason, Revelation & the Reconstitution of Rationality*, 126.

The Impact on Our Faith and Relationship with Allah

What is at stake here as well is our conception of God as living, active, and intimate. Abraham said to his father,

□يَا أَبَتِ لِمَ تَعْبُدُ مَا لَا يَسْمَعُ وَلَا يُبْصِرُ وَلَا يُغْنِي عَنكَ شَيْئًا□

> "Father, why do you worship that which does not hear and does not see and will not benefit you at all?" [Maryam 19:42]

Islam seeks to remove all intermediaries between humankind and God and make a person's heart attached only to Him. Those intermediaries are prevalent in the history of religion and philosophy, whether they are multiple gods, the trinity, or Neo-Platonist emanations. The attributes of God in Islam are clearly expressing a personal God to whom His creatures can relate and whom they can love, speak to with certainty that He hears them as they speak, and worship Him with certainty that He sees them as they bow, prostrate, and stand. The Prophet told us that He "faces the face of His servant as long as he does not turn away." It is an image of a God who constantly engages with His temporal creations; an efficient cause, not only final; an object of worship, not only wonderment: a God who is perpetually capable of doing what He pleases, as al-Fuḍayl (rA) said when they asked him about Allah's descent, "I believe in a Lord who does whatever He pleases."

Without a firm belief in the attribute of *ḥikmah* (wisdom) and its preponderant effect on the creation and creative will, our life in this world is subject to losing its meaning and moral significance. Moreover, beholding the various names and attributes of Allah adds to our recognition of Him and love for Him. Commenting on a statement by al-Harawi (rA), Ibn al-Qayyim (rA) wrote:

> Know that the intent of the sheikh and those like him of the people of uprightness is not for the heart to be focused on witnessing only one of the attributes, but it should rather attend to the *dhât* (ipseity) that is described by all attributes of perfection and majesty. Only then will its witnessing be of the *dhât* and attributes together. There is no doubt that this station is higher than witnessing one attribute alone. However, it may be said that witnessing one attribute alone stripped from the *dhât* is impossible, because in the extramental reality and even conceptually, it cannot be stripped from the *dhât*. In fact, once the heart witnesses the attribute, it simultaneously witnesses its subsistence in the (*dhât*) that is qualified by it. So, what then is the difference between witnessing the *dhât* and the attributes when it is all one and the same thing, which is that whosoever is more conscious of the attributes of Allah and more affirming of them, without any hindering

> misconceptions, will have a more complete *shuhood* (witnessing). Therefore, the one with the most complete *shuhood* is he who said, "I cannot count Your praises. You are as You have praised Yourself." Because of his full recognition of the names and attributes, he inferred from what he has known of them that the reality is beyond what he knew. Consciousness of the attributes is the way of the messengers and prophets and their inheritors. The more cognizant of them one is, the more knowing of Allah [one is]. Their witnessing is commensurate with what he has known of them. In reality, there is no real eye-witnessing of the *dhât* (ipseity) or the attributes; it is the strength of the servant's faith and certainty.[95]-[lv]

Someone may say, "Imam al-Nawawi's belief was not completely consistent with what you have presented, and it is highly unlikely that you had greater faith or better connection with Allah or *shuhood* of Him than he did." While the writer does not think for a minute otherwise, the fact that having complete acceptance of the reality of those names and attributes leads to better recognition of God and better relationship with Him is not compromised by this contention. In order for causes to lead to their desirable effects, they need to be complete causes and

---

[95] Shams al-Deen Muhammad ibn Abi Bakr Ibn Qayyim al-Jawziyyah, *Madârij al-Sâlikeen*, ed. Muhammad al-Baghdâdi (Beirut: Dâr al-Kitâb al-'Arabi, 1416/1996), 3:222.

there need to be no hindrances. For Imam al-Nawawi, there may have been a myriad of factors resulting in what we believe was an exceptional relationship with the Lord, and for this writer, there may be a myriad of hindrances keeping him from reaching those heights. Having said that, the Companions who had the greatest relationship with Allah never subjected the Divine attributes to any philosophical discourse or deflected their primary meanings for more esoteric ones. It is also because of the drying effect of rationalist theology on the heart that luminaries of the Sufi path like Imams al-Harawi and al-Jeelâni were vehemently opposed to it. It is their Sufism, in fact, more than their Ḥanbalism that caused them this aversion to it.

Our affirmation replaces the Christian immanence of God with His relatability. Our exoneration of the transcendent God replaces the philosophical apophatism with agnostic amodalism. The apparent meanings of the scriptural attributes of God are not anthropomorphic, they are anthropocentric. If we are the audience, should they be anything else?

□وَمَا جَعَلَهُ اللَّهُ إِلَّا بُشْرَىٰ لَكُمْ وَلِتَطْمَئِنَّ قُلُوبُكُم بِهِ □

> "And Allah made it not except as [a sign of] good tidings for you and to reassure your hearts thereby." ['Âl `Imrân 3:126]

WHAT ARE THE COUNTER ARGUMENTS?

Aside from some reports from the righteous predecessors that were understood by some scholars to mean *tafweeḍ* of meanings or even *ta'weel*, there are two groups of arguments that are cited by the negationists: conflict with reason and assimilating God to human beings (anthropomorphism) or other creations.

Reports from the *Salaf*

These may be instances where the predecessors contextually explained a verse or hadith by its ultimate implications or examples without negation of the apparent meanings, but their explanations later came to be viewed as *ta'weel* by some of the latter scholars among the rationalist theologians. They may also be statements about consigning the modality or ontological reality of the attributes to God that were later understood to mean consigning their meanings and lexical significations to God. We have discussed some of those reports in the section on the invalidity of *ta'weel* and *tafweeḍ al-ma'na*.

Conflict with Reason

The claimed conflict between reason and the primary meanings of the scriptural reports concerning the attributes is in fact a conflict between rational deliverances of certain philosophical schools that were prevalent at the time those controversies festered. As we explained in the section on epistemology, there is no real conflict between *a priori* knowledge that is recognized by human concurrence and any of those scriptural proofs. The two main rational arguments of the negationists are:

1. The perfect does not change and change is a sign of origination.
2. Composition and divisibility are signs of origination.

It is important to note here that Ahl al-Sunnah are affirmationists, so none of their scholars denied all attributes of God, but while the Mutakallimoon denied some (with major differences among them), the Atharis affirmed all. The following arguments may be used by any affirmationists against the negationists, whether they were Muslim scholars of Mu'tazili leaning, Muslim philosophers, heretical groups, or non-Muslims.

1. The Perfect Does Not Change

Aristotelians had great difficulty explaining change in the universe. As we mentioned at the beginning of this work, to Aristotle, the final cause, the unmoved mover, must be changeless, undifferentiated and undifferentiating, thus He does not instigate any new action or influence. How does change happen in the universe, then? This unmoved mover has the celestial spheres rotating in their place in wonderment of Him, without Him exerting any force on them, because, well, He must be changeless, and no succession of events can subsist in Him. He is pure actuality with no unactualized potential. The philosophers of this school have gone as far as denying God's knowledge of the particulars of this universe. To them, His knowledge of those changing particulars amounts to a relational change in His knowledge.

Aristotle believed in an eternal universe without beginning. His doctrines about God being a final cause, not an effective one, were consistent with his erroneous notion of the eternity of the universe. The notion that change cannot subsist in the Pre-Eternal is not a matter of agreement among the earlier philosophers, as Ibn Rushd (rA) asserts.[96] You can find in Plato's dialogues indications of that. He says, "Can we ever be made to believe that motion and life and soul are not present with perfect being [God]? Can we imagine that being is devoid of life and mind, and exists in awful unmeaningness, an everlasting fixture?"[97] Recently, the concept has been further

---

[96] Abu al-Waleed Muhammad Ibn Ahmad Ibn Rushd, *Tahâfut al-Tahâfut*, ed. Ṣalâḥ al-Deen al-Hawwâri (Beirut: al-Maktabah al-'Aṣriyyah, 1432/2011), 46-47.

challenged by many, like the evolutionary idealists in their understanding of the creative spirit.[98]

This concept of a static god of completely actualized potential makes it metaphysically impossible for that god to be effectively related to a changing world. It also seems to come into irreconcilable conflict with the Quranic description of God, as in the following verses and others:

□قُلِ اللَّهُ يَبْدَأُ الْخَلْقَ ثُمَّ يُعِيدُهُ□

> "Say, 'Allah begins creation and then repeats it'." [Yoonus 10:34]

□كُلَّ يَوْمٍ هُوَ فِي شَأْنٍ□

> "... every day He is bringing about a matter." [Al-Raĥmân 55:29]

□لَعَلَّ اللَّهَ يُحْدِثُ بَعْدَ ذَٰلِكَ أَمْرًا□

> "...perhaps Allah will bring about after that a [different] matter." [Al-Ṭalâq 65:1]

The temporality of creatures means that Allah has successive acts of creation. The Quran describes a God who engages with His temporal creations, time and again, as He wills, while acknowledging that time itself is His creation, so He is not bound by it, just as He is not bound by space. And while we agree that the essential attributes of the perfect and eternal are not subject to change, this should not mean that He may not be described by those

---

[97] Plato. *The Dialogues of Plato,* 4:380.

[98] H. A. Overstreet, "Change and the Changeless," *The Philosophical Review* 18, no. 1 (1909): 1, https://doi.org/10.2307/2177157.

Quranic accounts. The initiation of a certain action does not necessarily indicate a change of an attribute of the essence. His power is eternal, but its actualized deliverances happen in succession. They are still His. He is actively influencing every atom and every accident in His universe. None of this means a change of His essence, which is unbefitting of the Eternal without beginning or end, and there is no need to say that emergent events subsist in Him (*taḥullu feehi al-ḥawâdith*). These are not the scriptural terms. We will describe Him with the verses above and their like. This writer also believes that there is no reason to call the individual acts *ṣifât* (qualities/attributes) except in the sense that they could be predicated of God. Their species is *qadeem* (pre-eternal), and these are what could be described as qualities. And as Ibn al-Qayyim points out in *Madârij al-Sâlikeen*, even regarding the attributes of the face and hands, the disagreement over calling those predications "qualities" is a disagreement of form, not substance, and what matters is the amodal affirmation of their attribution to the Divine as He has stated in the Revelation.[99]-[lvi]

Imam Ibn Taymiyyah (rA) asserts that the people before Imam Ibn Kullâb (rA) were of two types: Ahl al-Sunnah, who affirmed the essential attributes (both rational and scriptural) and the volitional attributes, and

---

[99] Ibn Qayyim al-Jawziyyah, *Madârij al-Sâlikeen,* 3:323.

the Mu'tazilah, who denied both because of the concern about composition in the essence of God. Then, Ibn Kullâb approved of the first group and rejected the second. He was followed in this respect by Imam Abu al-Ḥasan al-Ashari (rA).[100]-[lvii]

What made the imams of *Mutakallimeen* deny those volitional attributes is, of course, not their blind following of Aristotle, but the fact that this was the prevalent philosophy of the time and they not only believed it, but they also used it to underpin their cosmological proof of God's existence. This theory proposes that accidents such as stillness and movement cannot simultaneously subsist in one entity, so they happen in succession, and thus must be originated, not eternal (the definitiveness of which al-Râzi [rA] himself denied, because as they may be eternal without end in paradise even while succeeding one another, it may be argued that they are also eternal in the past). Bodies (*ajsâm*) cannot exist without certain accidents (*a'râd*) such as movement and stillness, for instance. If so, and we have established that accidents are temporal not eternal, then all bodies are temporal as well, thus, the world originated at some point. This would then lead us to ask who originated it, and through *sabr* and *taqseem* (enumeration and division, or the process of

---

[100] Ibn Taymiyyah, *Dar' Ta'âruḍ al-'Aql wa al-Naql*, 2:6.

elimination) we can establish that God is the one who created it.

To the *Mutakallimeen*, this was their strongest rational proof regarding the creation of the universe by God. This means, though, that temporally originated accidents must not subsist in God, lest He be temporal, not eternal. This would lead to the denial of the volitional attributes. However, since it is impossible to deny the creation of things one after another, or the giving of life and death and providing, et cetera, the Mutakallimoon had a dilemma to solve. The Maturidis said that God has an eighth essential attribute, and they called it *takween* (genesis): a sort of eternal umbrella attribute for all those actions. The Ash'aris argued that those actions are not attributes, and they do not subsist in the *dhât* (ipseity) of God, but rather, the attribute of *qudrah* which is eternal has actualization relationality (*ta'alluq tanjeezi*) with its different actualizations in the particulars.

To Atharis, neither proposition provides a satisfactory answer, and neither solves the problem of His active creation and control. Calling it actualization relationality (*ta'alluq tanjeezi*) leaves us with a term that would still need to be qualified. Is this a mental conception or an extant reality outside the mind? If it is the first, it does not solve any problem in the extramental reality. If it is the second, it still attributes a relational change in the exercise of *qudrah*. Also, as Ibn Rushd (rA) stated, the issue that needs explanation is not the lag between the pre-eternal will and the creation of the universe, but rather between the act of creating by the Creator and the created coming into existence, particularly if the Creator is omnipotent. There is no way, he asserts, that the relationship between the Creator and the created at the time of creation is the same as it is at other times.[101] The only way to not concede to the philosophers' proposition about a "beginningless" world is by rejecting their conception of a god who is undifferentiated and undifferentiating, and affirming his volitional attributes. The concept of *ta'alluq tanjeezi* of the *qudrah* or the umbrella attribute of *takween* do not provide a satisfactory solution, no more so than do Philo's interpolation of the logos between God and the world and all of the emanationist theories, including the spiritual substances or "intelligences" Avicenna places between God and the world to explain how God can exercise temporal influence on His temporal creations.[102]

The Quran and the Sunnah abound with ascriptions of actions to God that happen in succession. Allah says,

□هُوَ الَّذِي خَلَقَ لَكُم مَّا فِي الْأَرْضِ جَمِيعًا ثُمَّ
اسْتَوَىٰ إِلَى السَّمَاءِ فَسَوَّاهُنَّ سَبْعَ سَمَاوَاتٍ □

[101] Ibn Rushd, *Tahâfut al-Tahâfut*, 48.

[102] James A. Arieti, and Patrick A. Wilson, *The Scientific & the Divine: Conflict and Reconciliation from Ancient Greece to the Present* (Lanham, MD: Rowman & Littlefield, 2003),158.

> "It is He who created for you all that which is on the earth. Then He directed Himself to the heaven, [His being above all creation,] and made them seven heavens." [Al-Baqarah 2:29]

> □وَلَقَدْ خَلَقْنَاكُمْ ثُمَّ صَوَّرْنَاكُمْ ثُمَّ قُلْنَا لِلْمَلَائِكَةِ اسْجُدُوا لِآدَمَ□

> "And We have certainly created you [O Humankind] and given you [human] form. Then We said to the angels, 'Prostrate to Adam'." [Al-A`râf 7:11]

The Quran describes a God that is actively creating and controlling every atom and accident of His creation. The matter is simple, in our belief, and the answer to the issue of change being a sign of origination lies in the following responses.

The belief in the attributes of voluntary actions that are mentioned throughout the Quran and the Sunnah is an affirmation of the perfection of the Lord and His omnipotence. It is essential for our perception of His relatability and presence, which are the Islamic counterparts of the Christian doctrine of immanence. If you give people a choice between a dynamic world and a static god, most will choose the dynamic world, because it is there affecting every moment of their lives.

The philosophers do not agree that any action of an agent necessitates a change in it.[103] We do not speak of change in God's essence, because that is unbefitting of the Eternal, and we do not speak of accidents subsisting in Him. We only affirm His actions as He spoke of them. Activity would necessarily mean change in the condition of the agent if he had to conform to the matter he is creating or reforming, or to exert effort to execute his volitions, such that "his acts are the expression of demands made upon him by conditions external to himself."[104] Imagine a tiller who must comply with the physical conditions of soil, nurture, sunshine, and so on.[105] If God, however, has infinite power, then His voluntary action is simply pure self-expression that is "concerned with nothing foreign or external to the self; it neither adds something not of the self to the self, nor makes something of the self into that which is not of the self."[106]

The rejection of change in perfect life is a product of the quantitative concept of God that is limited by the substance category. It is a limitation of the human mind which sees change as only disintegrative or augmentative, and then refuses to ascribe either to God. The question is whether we ought to apply those limitations to God. First, it is obvious that disintegrative and augmentative change is entirely unacceptable concerning God, because it means

---

[103] Ibn Rushd, *Tahâfut al-Tahâfut*, 47.

[104] Overstreet, "Change and the Changeless," 9.

[105] Ibid.

[106] Ibid, 11.

that he was not at some point perfect and then became perfect, or the opposite. However, none of those categories of human understanding bind God, so His voluntary actions do not need to be fitted into either type of change.

The inclusion of the "many activities" into the perfect one is not rejected by all philosophers. Hegel, for one, showed that this is possible as long as the many are "activities in a subject or spirit."[107] He went as far as stating that "A quality is a quality and nothing more; it belongs to the substance; an activity, on the contrary, is more than a particular activity; it is the subject."[108] His rejection of many qualities in a substance, when it comes to the perfect one, is based on the limitations of the substance category. We do not say that God is a substance, anyway. As for the distinction between activities and qualities, this writer believes that the individual acts of God are not other than God, but do not need to be described as qualities; the qualities are the species of those acts. His hearing the *mujâdilah* at the time she was talking to the Prophet is real, and while it is predicated of Him, it does not need to be described as a quality; the quality is the species, which is the Eternal hearing, of which His hearing this woman was a particular actualization.

---

[107] Ibid, 13.

[108] Ibid, 13.

The difficulty we have with the succession of events, and the reason some deny that a succession of events subsists in God, is that we cannot separate in our minds between the 'before' and the 'past' or the 'after' and the 'future' if the 'now' is the 'present.' The past, present, and future have different relations and values to us. But let us suppose that "the 'before' and the 'after' were all of equal clearness, equal intimacy, equal value...,"[109] will we have the same thoughts about the mere sequential succession? I think not. Well, we are certain that, to God, time is His creation and He encompasses it. There is no difference in value between the 'before' and the 'after.'

The proof of accidents and the origination of bodies is not the strongest proof for God's existence, let alone the only one. It is also not indubitable. Most philosophers believed in the "beginninglessness" of the universe; had it been an indubitable rational proof, it would have been obvious to the people endowed with intellect. However, the proof of change may be still used because the change in this universe is a change of the essence. Do you not see that we decompose and turn into dust, and the dust turns into plants which are eaten by animals? Change of the essence and essential attributes is not conceivable of the Eternal, but this does not preclude Him from engaging His creation temporally and effecting His eternal *qudrah* in

---

[109] Ibid, 13.

successive acts of creation, provision, giving life and death, and yes, *istiwâ'* and *nuzool* (descending).

Aside from that proof in itself, we may also say that we cannot infer from the *shahâdah* about the *ghayb*, so the principles applied to the universe through our empirical experience may not be applied to God.

﴿كُلَّ يَوْمٍ هُوَ فِي شَأْنٍ﴾

"... every day He is bringing about a matter."
[Al-Raĥmân 55:29]

The perfect essence does not change. God's activity is not a change of His essence.

2. The Composite god and Divisibility

Growing up in Egypt, some of my Christian classmates would tell me that we Muslims also have a trinity. They would argue that "In the name of Allah, the Most Merciful, Most Beneficent" recognizes a trinity. Even as a child, I felt that this argument was childish, but as I grew up, I discovered that this confusion between mental conceptions and ontological realities was not limited to my Christian classmates.

The notion of the simple (*baseeṭ*), undifferentiated God of Aristotle haunted some early Muslims; they came to be known as Jahmites and then Mu'tazilah. After all, we have an enormous emphasis in the Quran and the Sunnah on *tawḥeed* (the oneness of God). In order to adapt our concept of *tawḥeed* to the Aristotelian notion of the simple, undifferentiated God, some found it impossible for God to have any extant qualities (attributes) that are distinct from the Divine ipseity. They simply ignored the meaning of *tawḥeed* and *wâḥid* in the conventional use of the Arabic language and the Quran, and started to read Aristotle and Plotinus back into the Quran and the Sunnah and to project onto them their principles of God and conceptions of His unity. To avoid the problem of hypostasis and composition in the essence of God, the Jahmites felt that they needed to deny His names and attributes. The Mu'tazilah felt they had to deny the attributes, because if they are other than the ipseity (*dhât*), then they amount to hypostasis or composition, but they affirmed the names as mere names without the corresponding extant qualities (*ṣifât*). As a solitary (*aḥad*) extant deity, they argued, God must not have attributes distinct from the *dhât* (ipseity), so he does not have hearing, vision, or knowledge, but He hears, sees, and knows by His *dhât* (ipseity).

Whereas the earlier Mutakallimoon were more concerned about the volitional attributes because affirming them in their understanding meant the supervening of accidents in the Divine ipseity, which would mean His temporality and non-eternity, they affirmed the attributes of the *dhât*, such as the face, hands, and eyes, as we quoted before from Imam Abu al-Ḥassan himself and Imam al-Bâqillâni. They also affirmed Allah's aboveness in relation to the Throne. The latter Mutakallimoon, however, diverged from the earlier imams and invoked this principle about composition to deny certain attributes like Allah's aboveness in relation to the Throne. In the following segment, we will address that philosophical argument and attempt to show how part of it is baseless and the other part is not in conflict with the primary meanings of the scriptural attributes (*al-ṣifât al-khabariyyah*).

The very notion that having certain attributes that can be conceptualized distinctly from the *dhât* amounts to hypostasis and composition is totally absurd. It comes from Hellenic (ancient Greek) philosophies about the radical simplicity of the Divine. To any uncorrupted intellect, saying that He is omnipotent and omniscient does not amount to composition. No sane person who is not indoctrinated in a certain philosophical school would find a trinity here composed of the *dhât*, omnipotence, and omniscience.[110]-[lviii] Those attributes are not other than God; it is a fallacy, therefore, to claim that acknowledgment of these attributes is an acknowledgment of His *iftiqâr* (need of and dependence on) them. The one *dhât* (ipseity) and its essential

[110] Ibn Taymiyyah, *Dar' Ta'âruḍ al-'Aql wa al-Naql*, 1:281.

attributes are ontologically one indivisible entity, even if they can be conceptually separate. However, that concern about composition is exactly why the Jahimtes denied the names and attributes and that is why the Mu'tazilah denied the attributes. In fact, the epitome of this confusion between mental conceptions and ontological realities in the Aristotelian tradition of philosophy happens where it is posited that the quiddity (*mahiyya* or what-it-is-ness) is separate from existence (*wujood*), which must be added to it to have an extant being of this quiddity/essence. Applying this to the "First cause," the *wujood* (existence) would now be secondary to the quiddity, which is unbefitting of its firstness. So, it must have no quiddity! Some of them posited that the only quiddity of the "Necessary Existent" is its "being necessary." While these mental concepts are different, in the ontological reality there is no existence without quiddity and there is no omnipotence in the abstract, and no *dhât* that is completely devoid of all attributes; that is the description of *'adam* (nothingness).[111]

Until the time of the latter Mutakallimoon, Ahl al-Sunnah remained united against this form of *ta'ṭeel* (negationism) on the basis of this weak argument. However, the latter Mutakallimoon invoked this principle, albeit differently, to deny attributes other than the

---

[111] See al-Ghazâli, *Tahâfut al-Falâsifah*, 191.

essential ones. This brought about an avalanche of discord and dissension among Sunni Muslims, so it deserves some detailed treatment here, from my Athari viewpoint, of course.[112]

The main rational argument of the latter *Mutakallimeen* against Allah's *'uluw* and *istiwâ'* above the Throne is that if Allah is above the Throne, this means directionality (*jihah*), which means spatial locatedness (*taḥayyuz*), meaning that He would be occupying space (*ḥayyiz*), making Him a body (*jism*) subject to divisibility (*inqisâm*), which means that He is composed (*murakkab*), and also subject to need (*iftiqâr*) of His different parts, which are all impossible propositions; therefore, He is not above the Throne.[113]

The matter did not stop here, but as we have quoted from Imam al-'Izz, and as established in the books of the Mutakallimeen, they started to make all those propositions concomitants of each other, making one who believes in Allah's aboveness on the Throne a *kâfir*. This was according to those of them who would judge people by the *lawâzim* of their statements. While they exempted

---

[112] A non-Muslim academician may be less invested in this controversy, and so will likely address it from a more neutral perspective. This may not be possible or even desirable by us, as Muslims. However, what is both possible and desirable is to maintain a civil discourse and also maintain the love for those who sought the truth and were sincere in serving God and His *deen*.

[113] al-Râzi, *Asâs al-Taqdees*, 62-67.

the masses from this excommunication, as we explained in the section on epistemology, they did not extend the same exemption to the scholars. Due to various political, social, and intellectual reasons, within two centuries the Athari creed (whose protagonists, to be honest, were not particularly more lenient than the *Mutakallimeen*), became a marginal creed in certain parts of the Muslim world, and its followers were now under pressure to acquiesce or face defamation and persecution. If you take the aboveness of God in relation to the Throne to tell the story of that shift, we arrived at this point from a very long distance away, an (at least, tacit) agreement of the *salaf* on the affirmation, which is not only reported by Atharis like Imam Ibn 'Abd al-Barr, but also major Ash'aris like Imam al-Qurṭubi, who was impartial enough to say,

> Most of the early and latter [scholars] said, "When it is necessary to exonerate the Creator (*al-Bâri*) (Exalted is He) from directionality (*jihah*) and spatial locatedness (*taḥayyuz*), then it is a necessary concomitant of this, in the view of the majority of the early scholars and their later leaders, to exonerate Him from directionality. In their view, He is not in the direction of aboveness. This is because, to them, when Allah has a direction, this necessitates spatial locatedness (*makân*) and a confine (*ḥayyiz*), which necessitate movement and

stillness, and change and origination." This is the saying of the rationalist theologians. The early *salaf* (may Allah be pleased with them) never used to speak of the negation of direction , nor did they ever utter it. Rather, all of them spoke with affirmation of it (*jihah*) for Allah, the Exalted, just as His Book spoke of it and His Messengers told about it. None of the righteous predecessors (*al-Salaf al-Ṣâliḥ*) denied that He *istawa* (rose/settled) above His Throne in reality (*haqeeqatan*). And the Throne has been singled out because it is the greatest of His creations. The *salaf* had no knowledge of the *kayfiyyah* (modality) of *al-istiwâ'*, for there is no one who knows its ontological reality. Imam Mâlik (may Allah have mercy upon him) said, "*Al-istiwâ'* is known..." — meaning, in the language — "...and its modality is unknown, and asking about it is an innovation." Likewise, said Umm Salamah (may Allah be pleased with her).[114]-[lix]

Notice how Imam al-Qurṭubi (rA) candidly reports from all of the predecessors that they affirmed those attributes, and how he said that this means affirmation of the linguistic meanings, and that the only thing that is

---

[114] Abu 'Abd Allâh Muhammad ibn Ahmad al-Qurṭubi, *Tafseer al-Qurṭubi*, 2nd ed., ed. Ahmad al-Bardooni and Ibrâheem Aṭfayyish (Cairo: Dâr al-Kutub al-Miṣriyyah, 1384/1964), 7:219.

unknown (and consigned to God) is the modality. Notice how the following generations of Muslims, including the early *Mutakallimeen* like Imams Ibn Kullâb, Abu al-Hassan and al-Bâqillâni, continued to believe in this aboveness, as we have established. This was all based on myriad scriptural proofs without any diverting evidence from the scriptures, as Imam al-Taftazâni admitted.[115]

Now, in the sixth and seventh centuries, a new narrative was being forced on the collective consciousness of the Ummah, which blamed this creed on the Ḥanbalis and Karrâmites (who later became extinct). It did not stop there, but in modern times, to continue the character assassination of the opposition, the charge was narrowed down to Imam Ibn Taymiyyah, the first Ḥanbali to compose a rational rebuttal of *kalâm*'s propositions, in addition to the abundant scriptural proofs that were cited by the Atharis before. Now, to the extreme strands, you have a single person that can be blamed for this "heresy and disbelief" and, thus, they would spare no ammunition in brutalizing him. So, what caused all of this? Here are the links in the chain of argument espoused by the latter *Mutakallimeen*:

1. *'uluw* and *istiwâ'* entail directionality (*jihah*);

[115] al-Taftazâni, *Sharḥ al-Maqâṣid*, 3:36.

2. directionality (*jihah*) entails spatial locatedness (*taḥayyuz*);
3. spatial locatedness (*taḥayyuz*) entails corporealism (*tajseem*);
4. corporealism (*tajseem*) entails divisibility (*inqisâm*) and composition (*tarkeeb*); and
5. divisibility (*inqisâm*) and composition (*tarkeeb*) entail temporal origination (*ḥudooth*).

If this is the rational argument, there are three ways to address it: (1) to continue to cite the scriptures and the reported consensuses on the *'uluw* of Allah above His Throne, which is what the Ḥanbalis and other Atharis have always done; hence, the name *ḥashwiyyah* (people who 'stuff' their arguments with evidences they do not comprehend); (2) to leave out the scriptural evidences and mount a counter argument that is purely rational; or (3) to put together a systematic discourse in defense of the Athari creed that takes both scriptural and rational proofs into consideration and harmonizes them. The last is what Ibn Taymiyyah (rA) chose. He was a master of the transmitted and rational sciences, as acknowledged by his opponents, so he was best positioned to undertake this enormous task, which he believed would save the Islamic creed and reaffirm the epistemic primacy of the scriptures.

It would have been enough to break the chain mentioned above at one link, but what if we break it at several links? But, let us first acknowledge what we agree on.

We agree that Allah is not divisible or composed of parts. Ibn Taymiyyah (may Allah bestow mercy on him) said about the *ṣamadiyyah* of Allah, "Even if the created being may be *ṣamad* in certain respects, the reality of *ṣamadiyyah* does not exist in them, since they are subject to disunion and divisibility, and are also dependent on others."[116_lx]

And when he was answering the argument of Imam al-Râzi (rA), he stated:

> And there is no doubt that al-Râzi and those like him who use this proof do not explain *al-inqisâm* (divisibility) the way we have established: that of the separation of one part from another in that each part becomes in a separate distinct place, or the possibility of that [with respect to God]; for no one has said that Allah is divisible (*munqasim*) in this sense.[117_lxi]

Imam Ibn Taymiyyah was alluding to the other sense of *inqisâm*, which is between the ipseity and attributes, and He confirms that denying that meaning amounts to the

[116] Ibn Taymiyyah, *Majmoo' al-Fatâwa*, 17:238.

[117] Ibn Taymiyyah, *Bayân Talbees al-Jahmiyyah*, 3:440.

denial of any existence because there is no *dhât* that is not qualified by attributes.

Having said that, the general answer to this cascade of propositions is that it presumed similarity between what is known through our empirical senses (*shahâdah*) and what is beyond them (*ghayb*), particularly God. It once again comes back to the Kantian summons to the metaphysicians: is rational metaphysics rational? This is what our *salaf* always used in their refutation of the Jahmites who wanted to subject our theological discourse to the foreign discourse of the Peripatetics and Neoplatonists.

Here are some other detailed responses.

We agree that a perfect unity is not compatible with quantitative or aggregate unity. We agree that the perfect one cannot be of dissoluble nature, subject to disintegrative or augmentative change. We agree that the perfect cannot be made of parts that are separable and in need of each other. They are either adequate expressions of the whole, and in such case, we have multiplicity, or they are not, and in such case, they would not be perfect. We see that the limitations of human minds that are constrained by the substance category is what caused people to conflate the different attributes of God with the qualities of substances. Liberated from those confines, it will be possible to see that none of those attributes is in conflict with the concepts we agree on regarding God.

We do not use any of the terms used, including *jihah* (direction), *ḥayyiz* (spatial locatedness), *jism* (body), and the like, because they were not used in the Revelation, and terms that are foreign to it and can be given meanings *ad hoc* by different schools will create chaos if they were to dominate our theological discourse.

The word *jism* in the conventions of the Arabic language and the Quranic usage is totally inapplicable to God, as Ibn Taymiyyah stated. The problem is that they transfused the word with special technical definitions of the philosophers, who consider any entity of which attributes could be predicated and in which extant qualities may subsist, a body. If we reject God being a body in their sense of the word 'body,' we would be rejecting all His attributes. Most Muslims who used it (in error) did not ever mean that God is divisible, composed, or made of parts, but they meant that He subsists by Himself. That is how Imam Ibn Taymiyyah attempted to clarify their position, despite his rejection of it, to the Christian critics.[118]-lxii

Directionality means corporealism to some of us, only because we cannot think beyond our stiff categories of understanding. Imam Abu al-Hassan al-Ash'ari says in refutation of this,

---

[118] Ibn Taymiyyah, *al-Jawâb al-Ṣaḥeeḥ li man Baddala Deen al-Maseeḥ*, 4:430.

> It should be said to them, "Why did you assert that if the hand is not a favor, then it must be a limb?" If [in their response] they refer us to our empirical experience or to that which we witness in the creations and they say, "If the hand in that is not a favor, then it is a limb," it would be said to them, "If you infer from the empirical experience and judge Allah (the Exalted) on its basis, so likewise, we have not found a living being among the creations except that it is of flesh and blood, so affirm that for Allah (Exalted is He above that), otherwise, you would have abandoned your proposition and refuted your own argument. If you, instead, affirm (that God is) a living being not like any other living beings among us, then why do you deny that the two hands that Allah (the Exalted) has mentioned are neither favors nor limbs, and are unlike all other hands?"[119]-lxiii

In fact, Ibn Rushd (rA), the great jurist and most celebrated philosopher in Islamic history, denied that God's aboveness (*'uluw*), which is said to entail directionality (*jihah*), necessitates *taḥayyuz* and corporealism. Now, does he lack intellect? Whose intellect, then, is the measuring stick for which we will abandon the

[119] Abu al-Ḥassan 'Ali ibn Ismâ'eel al-Ash'ari, *al-Ibânah 'an Uṣool al-Diyânah*, ed. Fawqiyyah Ḥusayn Maḥmood (Cairo: Dâr al-Anṣâr, 1397H), 136.

obvious meanings of the scriptures and the agreement of the first community?

Imam Ibn Taymiyyah (rA) gives the parable of the *rooḥ* (spirit) and how it is described in the Quran to ascend and descend and how the Prophet says about it that the vision of the deceased follows it upon its ascension at the time of death. Are we going to call it a body? Some do. How do we define a body, then? It is known that people of sound reason differed on its definition. It does not appear from the scriptural usage of the word *jism* or *jasad* (body) that it would be called a body, yet it is described by all those attributes that this cascade of propositions presumes are to be only ascribed to bodies. The spirit, Ibn Taymiyyah adds, is described by all these attributes, even though it does not look anything similar to the bodies we see, and we cannot talk about its divisibility or other concomitants if we would like to call it a body. Furthermore, no matter whether we call it a body or not, it is only another of God's creations. How can we, then, subject Him (Exalted is He) to the same principles we are confined to because of our limited empirical experiences?[120-lxiv]

The same argument the Mutakallimoon are using to deny some attributes is used against them by the Mu'tazilah and philosophers to deny all attributes. After all, there is nothing beyond substances and accidents in

---

[120] Ibn Taymiyyah, *Majmoo' al-Fatâwa*, 3:33.

our experience, and anything that has "attributes" subsist in it must be a substance, the philosophers claim. They would also claim that nothing other than bodies may be described as hearing and seeing, or even alive.[121-lxv]

Additionally, who said that every *jism* (a term we do not use for God) is divisible? This is all based on Aristotelian atomism. So, to them, a corpus that is free of composition (*tarkeeb*) must be the minute and insignificant individual atom (*al-jawhar al-fard*).[122] However, the philosophers themselves do not agree on the notion that all bodies are composed of the individual atoms. Some, including idealists like Berkeley,[123] do not even acknowledge any material existence. Scientifically, we know now that even the nucleus of an atom can be split, and that matter and energy are completely interchangeable. To scientists, this is now established. Not only this, but matter, energy, space, and time are all presumed to be interchangeable, implying to some that they are all one thing and everything around us is simply subjective relationships. But more importantly, why are we applying any of this to God?

Also, who said that every composed being needs a composer? The philosophers. When Imam al-Ghazâli (rA)

---

[121] Ibn Taymiyyah, *Dar' Ta'âruḍ al-'Aql wa al-Naql*, 6:127.

[122] al-Râzi, *Asâs al-Taqdees*, 62-67.

[123] George Berkeley (pronounced BARK-ly; 1685– 1753 CE) was an Irish Anglican philosopher.

was attempting to refute their argument, he said, "Your saying that every *murakkab* (composed entity) needs a *murakkib* (composer) is like someone saying every *mawjood* (extant entity) needs a *mujid* (maker)."[124]-[lxvi] Then he proceeded to say that the First cannot be a body, not because of this argument of composition, but rather, because accidents subsist in bodies, as we explained in the *kalâm* argument for the origination of bodies in the last section.

Moreover, who said that composed bodies must be temporally originated? The imams of the *kalâm* scholars. However, if this is meant to be a decisive rational argument, how come it did not convince the vast majority of philosophers who believe in the beginningless eternity of the universe?

Finally, do we really need convoluted forms of the simple cosmological argument of the Quran?

□أَمْ خُلِقُوا مِنْ غَيْرِ شَيْءٍ أَمْ هُمُ الْخَالِقُونَ. أَمْ خَلَقُوا
السَّمَاوَاتِ وَالْأَرْضَ ۚ بَل لَّا يُوقِنُونَ. أَمْ عِندَهُمْ
خَزَائِنُ رَبِّكَ أَمْ هُمُ الْمُصَيْطِرُونَ.□

"Or were they created by nothing, or were they the creators [of themselves]? Or did they create the heavens and the earth? Rather, they are not certain. Or have they the depositories [containing the provision] of

[124] al-Ghazâli, *Tahâfut al-Falâsifah*, 176.

your Lord? Or are they the controllers [of them]?" [Al-Ṭoor 52:54-56]

As Imam al-Khaṭṭâbi said, the argument keeps getting more difficult.[125] Then, Allah switches the argument to allude to the necessity of this arrhythmic universe being controlled by someone who is willful, not a mechanical process of nature.

Ibn Taymiyyah (rA) provides a simpler explanation of the cosmological argument that rests on three pillars: the existence of extant beings that are obviously temporal, like ourselves, for example, and that are incapable of creation themselves. This points to a creator. The Creator must be an uncaused cause, eternal and self-sufficient, otherwise we fall in infinite regression. Also, the possible/contingent creations (*mumkin*) need a preponderator who is necessary (*wâjib al-wujood*) to come to existence, and since the *mumkin* is existent, the necessary is, *a priori*, existent.[126-lxvii] Now, complicating the argument does not seem to earn us more subscribers. As we have seen before, the more convoluted argument of the "accidents and origination of bodies" had opposition, even from the *kalâm* scholars themselves. Those who will not see the argument presented by the Quran and pointed out by the messengers since the beginning of humanity will not be

---

[125] Ibn Ḥajar, *Fatḥ al-Bâri*, 8:603.

[126] Ibn Taymiyyah, *Majmoo' al-Fatâwa*, 3:9.

convinced by the controversial products of human intellect; they need to be advised to rehabilitate their *fiṭrah* through spiritual labor before benefiting from an intellectual inquiry of this magnitude and consequentiality.

Anthropomorphism and Assimilation

As said in the introduction, the charge of anthropomorphism will continue to be directed at all religions, let alone the believers in the attributes of God mentioned in the Torah, Gospel, and the Quran. In the same article we quoted at the beginning of this piece, Peter Westh wrote, "First, underlying the general bias toward animism and anthropomorphism is a bias toward attributing and inferring *agency* – in Barrett's terms, the human mind is endowed with a Hyperactive Agency Detection Device."[127] It is thus a charge against people who believe in an intentional supreme agent, and there will be no way to avoid this unless one disbelieves in a God that is willful, or does not believe in a God at all.

Anthropomorphism is about likening God to humans and assimilation is about likening God to anything else, so the second term is more general and comprehensive, and it is the appropriate word to convey the meaning of *tashbeeh* in our Islamic tradition. The same argument used by *Mutakallimeen* against Atharis is used by the Mu'tazilah

---

[127] Westh, "Anthropomorphism in God Concepts," 396–414.

against *Mutakallimeen*, and by the pure Jahmites, Qarmatians, and some philosophers against the Mu'tazilah. In my view, the choice is between rejecting the argument at the outset and using nominalism and amodalism to deny the charge of assimilation, or a full retreat to negative theology and the denial of any Divine attributes or knowledge of the Divine. In fact, it is denial of the existence of the Divine that will be the only way to be clear of assimilation in the eyes of the radical accusers, because for any two things that exist, there must be something in common (*qadr mushtarak*), which is that each exists.

Detailed answers to the charge of anthropomorphism have been discussed throughout this work: for instance, the earlier discussion on the common degree (*al-qadr al-mushtarak*). However, if one thing needs reiteration, I would say that the reason the Revelation used language that, to some, implied assimilation is the need to address us humans according to our categories of understanding. If the Revelation were to avoid, in telling us about the *ghayb*, using any language that is ordinarily used to describe matters within the realm of our empirical experience, it would have not told us anything about it, simply because human language was developed in the first place to denote things and concepts humans experience in the world of *shahâdah*. The formula of moderation is given to us by God, where He says,

□لَيْسَ كَمِثْلِهِ شَيْءٌ ۖ وَهُوَ السَّمِيعُ الْبَصِيرُ□

"There is nothing like unto Him, and He is the Hearing, the Seeing." [Al-Shoorâ 42:11]

CONCLUSION

Ontologically, no extant being lacks quiddity and attributes. Noumenally, the apophatic god is nonexistent, and phenomenally, it cannot be felt or related to, let alone loved and worshipped. In conclusion of this work, here are my recommendations:

- To be deserving of Divine guidance, we need to purify our intentions by true devotion to Allah. We also need to constantly rehabilitate our *fiṭrah* and heal it from the ills of bias (*hawa*), ulterior motives (*aghrâḍ*), blind imitation (*taqleed*), habit (*'âdah*), and conjecture (*gharṣ*). This can only be done through spiritual labor and immersion in the Revelation as understood and practiced by the first community.
- We must not subject the Divine instruction to prevalent intellectual or social conventions or transplant xenografts and foreign discourses into our hermeneutical system. We must affirm our belief in the epistemic superiority and self-sufficiency of the Revelation as the ultimate source of truth about the unseen. This will never

require us to impugn the office of reason or undercut its value in understanding the Revelation and defending its doctrines.

- Our belief in Allah must be rooted in His exoneration from all deficiencies and His absolute incomparability (*tanzeeh*), and the amodal affirmation (*ithbât*) of His attributes by which He has described Himself and His Messenger described Him. In our affirmation of the Divine attributes, we should never accept the so-called "necessary concomitants." Inferring from the world of *shahâdah* (seen) about the world of *ghayb* (unseen) is both irrational and perilous.
- We must be respectful of the imams of this *deen*, regardless of our agreement or disagreement with them. When we have to disagree, we must continue to love those who spent their lives serving Allah and His cause, and show them the requisite respect.
- The public should be spared the confusion of intra-Islamic polemics on creed and taught the basics of *'aqeedah* that will provide them with enough guardrails. People should then be uplifted spiritually to *want* to seek Allah and earn His pleasure. When it comes to the Divine attributes, teachers must prime their

understanding with *tanzeeh* and let the rhetorical strength and richness of the Revelation flow to their hearts, unimpeded by intellectual objections.

BIBLIOGRAPHY AND WORKS CITED

N.B.: The books of hadith are not mentioned in this bibliography because of the ease of locating the different hadith narrations.

1. Abu Ḥanifah, al-Nu'mân ibn Thâbit. *al-Fiqh al-Akbar*. UAE: Maktabat al-Furqân, 1419/1999.

2. Abu Ya'la, Muhammad ibn al-Ḥusayn ibn al-Farrâ'. *Ibṭâl al-Ta'weelât li Akhbâr al-Ṣifât*. Edited by Muhammad ibn Ḥamad al-Najdi. Kuwait: Dar Eelâf, n.d.

3. Aṣbahâni (al-), Abu al-Qâsim Ismail ibn Muhammad. *Al-Ḥujjah fi Bayân al-Maḥajjah*. 2nd ed. Edited by Muhammad ibn Rabee' al-Madkhali. Riyadh: Dâr al-Râyah, 1419/1999.

4. Arieti, James A. and Patrick A. Wilson, *The Scientific & the Divine: Conflict and Reconciliation from Ancient Greece to the Present*. Lanham, MD: Rowman & Littlefield, 2003.

5. Ash'ari (al-), Abu al-Ḥasan 'Ali ibn Ismâ'eel. *Al-Ibânah 'an Uṣool al-Diyânah*. Edited by Fawqiyyah Ḥusayn Maḥmood. Cairo: Dâr al-Anṣâr, 1397H.

6. Ash'ari (al-), Abu al-Ḥasan 'Ali ibn Ismâ'eel. *Maqâlât al-Islâmiyeen*. 3rd ed. Edited by Hellmut Ritter. Wiesbaden: Franz Steiner, 1400/1980.

7. Bâqillâni (al-), Abu Bakr Muhammad ibn al-Ṭayyib. *Tamheed al-Awâ'il wa Talkheeṣ al-Dalâ'il*. Edited by 'Imâd al-Deen Ahmad Ḥaydar. Beirut: Mu'assasat al-Kutub al-Thaqâfiyyah, 1407/1987.

8. Bayhaqi (al-), Ahmad ibn al-Ḥusayn. *Al-Sunan al-Kubrâ*. 3rd ed. Edited by Muhammad 'Abd al-Qâdir 'Aṭa. Beirut: Dâr al-Kutub al-'Ilmiyyah, 1424/2003.

9. Black, Deborah L. "Al-Farabi." In *History of Islamic Philosophy*, edited by Seyyed Hossein Nasr and Oliver Leaman, 178-197. London & New York: Routledge, 2001.

10. Chase, Michael. From the four Aristotelian questions to tawḥīd: Notes on the origins of negative theology in Islam. (Academic article published online, c. 2017). Retrieved from

https://www.academia.edu/39185335/From_the_four_Aristotelian_questions_to_tawḥīd_Notes_on_the_origins_of_negative_theology_in_Islam

11. Dardeer (al-), Ahmad ibn Ahmad. *Sharḥ al-Khareedah al-Bahiyyah.* Edited by 'Abd al-Salâm ibn 'Abd al-Hâdi. Istanbul: Dâr al-Bayrooti, 2015.

12. Dârimi (al-), Abu Sa'eed 'Uthmân ibn Sa'eed. *Naqḍ al-Imâm Abi Sa'eed al-Dârimi 'ala al-Ma'eesi.* Edited by Rasheed ibn Hassan al-Alma'i. Riyadh: Maktabat al-Rushd, 1418/1998.

13. Dhahabi (al-), Shams al-Deen Muhammad ibn Ahmad. *Al-'Arsh.* Madinah: Islamic University, 1424/2003.

14. Dhahabi (al-), Shams al-Deen Muhammad ibn Ahmad. *Siyar A'lâm al-Nubalâ'.* Cairo: Dâr al-Ḥadeeth, 1427/2006.

15. El-Tobgui, Carl Sharif. *Reason, Revelation & the Reconstitution of Rationality: Taqī Al-Dīn Ibn Taymiyya's (d. 728/1328)* "Dar' Ta'ārud Al-Aql Wa-l-Naql" *or "The Refutation of the Contradiction of Reason and Revelation."* Montreal: McGill University Libraries, 2013.

16. Ghazâli (al-), Abu Ḥâmid Muhammad ibn Muhammad. *Iḥyâ' 'Uloom al-Deen*. Beirut: Dâr al-Ma'rifah, n.d.

17. Ghazâli (al-), Ahu Ḥâmid Muhammad ibn Muhammad. *Tahâfut al-Falâsifah*. 6th ed. Edited by Sulaymân Dunya. Cairo: Dâr al-Ma'ârif, n.d.

18. Hakim, Ajhar A. "The Forgotten Rational Thinking in the Ḥanbalite Thought With Special Reference to Ibn Taymiyya." *Journal of Arabic and Islamic Studies* 14, no. 1 (2014): 137. https://doi.org/10.5617/jais.4642.

19. Haytami (al-), Ahmad ibn Muhammad ibn Ḥajar. *Tuḥfat al-Muḥtâj fi Sharḥ al-Minhâj*. Cairo: al-Maktabah al-Tijariyyah al-Kubra, 1357/1983.

20. Holtzman, Livnat. "Accused of Anthropomorphism: Ibn Taymiyya's Miḥan as Reflected in Ibn Qayyim Al-Jawziyya's *al-Kāfiya al-Shāfiya*." *The Muslim World* 106, no. 3 (2016): 561–87. https://doi.org/10.1111/muwo.12153.

21. Holtzman, Livnat. "'Does God Really Laugh?' – Appropriate and Inappropriate Descriptions of God in Islamic Traditionalist Theology." *Laughter in the Middle Ages and Early Modern Times Fundamentals of Medieval*

and Early Modern Culture, 2010, Chapter 2, 165–200. https://doi.org/10.1515/9783110245486.165

22. Hoover, Jon. *Ibn Taymiyya's Theodicy of Perpetual Optimism*. Leiden: Brill, 2007. https://doi.org/10.1163/ej.9789004158474.i-270.

23. Ibn 'Abd al-Barr, Abu 'Umar Yoosuf ibn 'Abd Allâh al-Namari. *Al-Tamheed lima fil-Muwa□□â' min al-Ma'âni wal-Asâneed*. Edited by Muṣṭafâ ibn Ahmad al-'Alawi and Muhammad 'Abd al-Kabeer al-Bakri. Morocco: Ministry of Endowments and Islamic Affairs, 1967.

24. Ibn 'Arabi, Muḥyee al-Deen Muhammad ibn Ali. *Al-Futuḥât al-Makkiyyah*. Beirut: Dâr al-Kutub al-'Ilmiyyah, n.d.

25. Ibn 'Eesa, Ahmad ibn Ibrâheem. Edited by Zuhayr al-Shaweesh. *Tawḍeeḥ al-Maqâṣid wa Taṣḥeeḥ al-Qawâ'id fi Sharḥ Qaṣeedat ibn al-Qayyim al-Kâfiyah al-Shâfiyah*, 3rd ed. Beirut: al-Maktab al-Islâmi, 1406H.

26. Ibn 'Abd al-Salâm, 'Izz al-Deen. *Qawâ'id al-Aḥkâm*. Edited by Ṭâha 'Abd al-Ra'oof Sa'd. Cairo: Maktabat al-Kulliyât al-Azhariyyah, n.d.

27. Ibn Ḥajar al-'Asqalâni. *Fatḥ al-Bâri fi Sharḥ Ṣaḥeeḥ al-Bukhâri*. Beirut: Dâr al-Ma'rifah, 1959.

28. Ibn Ḥanbal, Ahmad. *Al-'Aqeedah, Riwâyat Abi Bakr al-Khallâl*. Edited by 'Abd al-'Azeez al-Sayrawan. Damascus: Dâr Qutaybah, 1408.

29. Ibn Katheer, Abu al-Fidâ' Ismail ibn Umar. *Tafseer al-Quran al-'Aẓeem*. Edited by Muhammad Ḥusayn Shams al-Deen. Beirut: Dâr al-Kutub al-'Ilmiyyah, 1419H.

30. Ibn Qayyim al-Jawziyyah, Shams al-Deen Muhammad ibn Abi Bakr. *Mukhtaṣar al-Ṣawâ'iq al-Mursalah 'ala al-Jahmiyyah wa al-Mu'aṭṭilah*. Abbreviated by Ibn al-Muṣili Muhammad ibn 'Abd al-Kareem al-Ba'li. Cairo: Dâr al-Ḥadeeth, 1422/2001.

31. Ibn Qayyim al-Jawziyyah, Shams al-Deen Muhammad ibn Abi Bakr. *Madârij al-Sâlikeen*. Edited by Muhammad al-Baghdâdi. Beirut: Dâr al-Kitâb al-'Arabi, 1416/1996.

32. Ibn Rajab, Zayn al-Deen 'Abd al-Rahman. *Rawâi' al-Tafseer: al-Jâmi' li Tafseer al-Imâm Ibn Rajab al-Ḥanbali*. Edited by Abu Mu'âdh Ṭâriq ibn 'Awaḍ Allâh. Riyadh: Dâr al-'Âṣimah, 1422/2001.

33. Ibn Rushd, Abu al-Waleed Muhammad Ibn Ahmad. *Faṣl al-Maqâl wa-Taqreer ma bayn al-Ḥikmah wa al-*

Sharee'ah min Ittiṣâl. 2nd ed. Edited by Muhammad 'Umârah. Cairo: Dar al-Ma 'ârif, n.d.

34. Ibn Taymiyyah, Ahmad ibn 'Abd al-Ḥaleem ibn 'Abd al-Salâm. *Al-Musawwadah.* Edited by Muhamamd Muḥyi al-Deen 'Abd al-Ḥameed. Beirut: Dâr al-Kitâb al-'Arabi, n.d.
35. Ibn Taymiyyah, Taqi al-Deen Ahmad ibn 'Abd al-Ḥaleem. *Bayân Talbees al-Jahmiyyah.* Madinah: Mujamma' al-Malik Fahd li Ṭibâ'at al-Muṣḥaf al-Shareef, 1426H.
36. Ibn Taymiyyah, Taqi al-Deen Ahmad ibn 'Abd al-Ḥaleem. *Dar' Ta 'âruḍ al- 'Aql wa al-Naq*l. 2nd ed. Edited by Muhamamd Rashâd Sâlim. Riyadh: Mohammad Ibn Saud Islamic University, 1411/1991.
37. Ibn Taymiyyah, Taqi al-Deen Ahmad ibn 'Abd al-Ḥaleem. *Al-Jawâb al-Ṣaḥeeḥ li man Baddala Deen al-Maseeḥ.* 2nd ed. Edited by 'Ali ibn Hassan, 'Abd al-'Azeez ibn Ibrâheem and Ḥamdân ibn Muhammad. Riyadh: Dâr al-'Âṣimah, 1419/1999.

38. Ibn Taymiyyah, Taqi al-Deen Ahmad ibn 'Abd al-Ḥaleem. *Majmoo' al-Fatâwa*. 2nd ed. Edited by 'Abd al-Raḥmân ibn Qâsim al-Najdi. 20 vols. Cairo: Maktabat Ibn Taymiyyah, n.d.

39. Jeelâni (al-), 'Abd al-Qâdir. *al-Ghunyah*. 2nd ed. Edited by Salâḥ ibn Muhammad ibn 'Uwaydah. Beirut: Dâr al-Kutub al-'Ilmiyyah, 1417/1997.

40. Juwayni (al-), Abu al-Ma'âli 'Abd al-Malik. *Al- 'Aqeedah al-Nizâmiyyah.* Edited by M. Zâhid al-Kawthari. Cairo: al-Maktabah al-Azhariyyah lil-Turâth, 1412H.

41. Juwayni (al-), Abu al-Ma'âli 'Abd al-Malik. *al-Irshâd*. Cairo: Maktabat al-Thaqâfah al-Deeniyyah, 2015.

42. Juwayni (al-), Abu al-Ma'âli 'Abd al-Malik. *al-Irshâd*. Cairo: Maṭba'at al-Sa'âdah, 1369H.

43. Kant, Immanuel. *Critique of Pure Reason*. Translated and edited by Paul Guyer and Allen W. Wood. Cambridge, 1999.

44. Kars, Aydogan. "Unsaying God: Negative Theology in Medieval Islam". New York: Oxford University Press, 2019. Oxford Scholarship Online, 2019. https://doi.org/10.1093/oso/9780190942458.001.0001.

45. Khaṭṭâbi (al-), Abu Sulaymân Ḥamd ibn Muhamma. *Ma 'âlim al-Sunan*. Aleppo: al-Maṭba'ah al-'Ilmiyyah, 1351/1932.

46. Michot, J. Yahya. "A Mamlūk Theologian's Commentary on Avicenna's *Risāla Aḍḥawiyya*, being a translation of a part of the *Dar' al-Ta'āruḍ* of Ibn Taymiyya, with introduction, annotation, and appendices." *Journal of Islamic Studies* 14, no. 2 (2003): 149–203.

47. Nawawi (al-), Yaḥyâ ibn Sharaf. *Ṣaḥeeḥ Muslim bi-Sharḥ al-Nawawi*. Beirut: Dar Ihyâ' al-Turâth al-'Arabi, 1972.

48. Overstreet, H. A. "Change and the Changeless." *The Philosophical Review* 18, no. 1 (1909): 1. https://doi.org/10.2307/2177157.

49. Plato. *The Dialogues of Plato: in Five Volumes*. Translated by Benjamin Jowett. Oxford: Clarendon Press, 1953.

50. Qurṭubi (al-), Abu 'Abd Allâh Muhammad ibn Ahmad. *Tafseer al- Qurṭubi*. 2nd ed. Edited by Ahmad al-Bardooni and Ibrâheem Aṭfayyish. Cairo: Dâr al-Kutub al-Miṣriyyah, 1384/1964.

51. Râzi (al-), Fakhr al-Deen. *Asâs al-Taqdees.* Edited by Ahmad Hijâzi al-Saqqa. Cairo: Maktabat al-Kulliyyât al-Azhariyyah, 1406/1986.

52. Sanoosi (al-), Muhammad ibn Yoosuf. *Sharḥ al-'Aqeedah al-Kubrâ.* Edited by al-Sayyid Yoosuf Ahmad. Beirut: Dâr al-Kutub al-'Ilmiyyah, 2006.

53. Ṭabari (al-), Muhammad ibn Jareer. *Al-Tabṣeer fi Ma'âlim al-Deen.* Edited by 'Ali ibn 'Abd al-'Azeez al-Shibl. Riyadh: Dâr al-'Âṣimah, 1416/1996.

54. Taftazâni (al-), Sa'd al-Deen Mas'ood ibn 'Umar. *Sharḥ al-Maqâṣid.* Edited by Ibrâheem Shams al-Deen. Beirut: Dâr al-Kutub al-'Ilmiyyah, 2010.

55. Ibn Rushd, Abu al-Waleed Muhammad Ibn Ahmad. *Tahâfut al-Tahâfut.* Edited by Ṣalâḥ al-Deen al-Hawwâri. Beirut: al-Maktabah al- 'Aṣriyyah, 1432/2011.

56. Tirmidhi (al-), Abu 'Eesa, Muhammad ibn 'Eesa. *Sunan al-Tirmidhi.* Edited by Bashshâr 'Awwâd Ma'roof. Beirut: Dâr al-Gharb al-Islâmi, 1998.

57. Westh, Peter. "Anthropomorphism in God Concepts: The Role of Narrative." In *Origins of Religion, Cognition*

and Culture. Edited by Armin Geertz, 396–414. Abingdon, UK: Routledge, 2007.

GLOSSARY OF ARABIC TERMS

Ahl al-Sunnah wa al-Jamâ'ah	'People of the Sunnah and the Community'; also called *Ahl al-Sunnah* for short
'aqeedah	creed
Ash'ari	intellectual tradition in matters of creed that subscribes to the teachings of Imam Abu al-Ḥasan al-Ash'ari
Athari	scripturalist
badeehi	*a priori*
ḍaroori	compelling
deen	religion, way of life
dhât	ipseity; selfhood
fatwa (*fatwâ*)	expert opinion; religious edict
fiṭrah	original disposition
ghayb	what is not perceivable by the senses, unseen
ḥadd	spatial extent; limit
ḥaqeeqah	literal, truth
ḥawâdith	(sg. *ḥâdith*) events, originated

	things
ḥiss	sense, perception
'ibâdah	worship
ilhâm	inspiration
'ilm	knowledge; certainty
istiwâ'	ascension; establishment
jihah	direction, directionality
jism	substance, body, corpus
kâfir	disbeliever
kalâm	(*lit.* speech) rational theology
lawâzim	(sg. *lâzim*) necessary concomitants
Mutakallimoon, Mutakallimeen	(sg. *mutakallim*) rationalist theologians
Mu'tazilah	a major rationalist school
qadeem	pre-eternal
qudrah	power
salaf	predecessors
al-salaf al-ṣâliḥ	the righteous predecessors
shahâdah	objects of the senses, seen
ṣifât	(sg. *ṣifah*) attributes, qualities
tâbi'oon/ tâbi'een	'successors': those believers who met any of the Prophet's Companions
tafweeḍ al-	consigning the modality or ontological reality to God

kayf	
tafweeḍ al-ma'na; tafweeḍ	consigning the meaning to God
tajseem	corporealism
takfeer	excommunication, declaring s.o. a disbeliever
tanzeeh	God's transcendence and incomparability
taqleed	blind following or imitation
taṣawwuf	Sufism
tashbeeh	assimilation
ta'ṭeel	negation
ta'weel	figurative interpretation, reinterpretation
tawḥeed	recognition and affirmation of the oneness of God
'uluw	aboveness
Ummah	community or nation, the entire global community of Muslims
wâjib al-wujood	necessary existent
walâ'	religious allegiance and love
ẓanni	speculative (from *ẓann*: conjecture)

ẓawâhir (sg. *ẓâhir*) apparent or primary meanings

NOTES IN ARABIC

[i]الذهبي في السير: ومن كَفَّر ببدعة، وإن جلت، ليس هو مثل الكافر الأصلي، ولا اليهودي والمجوسي؛ أبى الله أن يجعل من آمن بالله ورسوله واليوم الآخر وصام وصلى وحج وزكى، وإن ارتكب العظائم وضل وابتدع، كمن عاند الرسول وعبد الوثن ونبذ الشرائع وكفر؛ ولكن نبرأ إلى الله من البدع وأهلها.

[ii]العز في قواعد الأحكام: فكذلك لا يكون اختلاف المسلمين في صفات الإله اختلافا في كونه خالقهم وسيدهم المستحق لطاعتهم وعبادتهم. وكذلك اختلف قوم في صفات أبيهم، مع اتفاقهم على أنه أصلهم الذي خلقوا من مائه، ولا يكون اختلافهم في أوصافه اختلافا في كونهم نشئوا عنه وخلقوا منه. فإن قيل: يلزم من الاختلاف في كونه سبحانه في جهة أن يكون حادثا؟ قلنا: لازم المذهب ليس بمذهب، لأن المجسمة جازمون بأنه في جهة وجازمون بأنه قديم أزلي ليس بمحدث، فلا يجوز أن ينسب إلى مذهب من يصرح بخلافه، وإن كان لازما من قوله. والعجب أن الأشعرية اختلفوا في كثير من الصفات كالقدم والبقاء والوجه واليدين والعينين، وفي الأحوال كالعالمية والقادرية، وفي تعدد الكلام واتحاده، ومع ذلك لم يكفر بعضهم بعضا، واختلفوا في تكفير نفاة الصفات مع اتفاقهم على كونه حيا قادرا سميعا بصيرا متكلما، فاتفقوا على كماله بذلك واختلفوا في تعليله بالصفات المذكورة.

[iii]ابن تيمية في الدرء: أيضا فالحس نوعان: حس ظاهر يحسه الإنسان بمشاعره الظاهرة، فيراه ويسمعه ويباشره بجلده، وحسن باطن كما أن الإنسان يحس بما في باطنه من اللذة والألم والحب والبغض والفرح والحزن والقوة والضعف وغير ذلك. والروح تحس بأشياء لا يحس بها البدن، كما يحس من يحصل له نوع تجريد بالنوم وغيره بأمور لا يحس بها غيره. ثم الروح بعد الموت تكون أقوى تجردا، فترى بعد

الموت وتحس بأمور لا تراها الآن ولا تحس بها. وفي الأنفس من يحصل له ما يوجب أن يرى بعينه ويسمع بأذنه ما لا يراه الحاضرون ولا يسمعونه، كما يرى الأنبياء الملائكة ويسمعون.

[iv] ابن تيمية في المسودة في أصول الفقه: مذهب أصحابنا أن أخبار الآحاد المتلقاة بالقبول تصلح لإثبات أصول الديانات.

[v] ابن عبد البر في التمهيد: وقال قوم كثير من أهل الأثر وبعض أهل النظر إنه يوجب العلم الظاهر والعمل جميعا، منهم الحسين الكرابيسي وغيره، وذكر ابن خوازِ بَنداذ أن هذا القول يخرج على مذهب مالك. قال أبو عمر: الذي نقول به إنه يوجب العمل دون العلم كشهادة الشاهدين والأربعة سواء. وعلى ذلك أكثر أهل الفقه والأثر، وكلهم يدين بخبر الواحد العدل في الاعتقادات ويعادي ويوالي عليها ويجعلها شرعا ودينا في معتقده؛ على ذلك جماعة أهل السنة، ولهم في الأحكام ما ذكرنا، وبالله توفيقنا.

[vi] أبو يعلى في إبطال التأويلات: قال أبو بكر الخلال: رأيت فِي كتاب لهرون المستملي أنه قال لأبي عبد الله: حديث جابر بن عبد الله "ضحك ربنا حتى بدت لهواته أو قال أضراسه" ممن سمعته؟ قال: نا روح، قال رسول الله – صلى الله عليه وسلم: "يضحك حتى بدت لهواته أو قال أضراسه" فقد نص على صحة هذه الأحاديث والأخذ بظاهرها والإنكار على من فسرها، وذلك أنه ليس في حمله على ظاهره ما يحيل صفاته ولا يخرجها عما نستحقه، لأنا لا نثبت ضحكا هو فتح الفم وتكشير شفتين وأسنان، ولا نثبت أضراسا ولهوات هي جارحة ولا أبعاضا، بل نثبت ذلك صفة كما أثبتنا الوجه واليدين والسمع والبصر، وإن لم نعقل معناه، ولا يجب أن نستوحش من إطلاق هذا اللفظ إذا ورد به سمع، كما لا نستوحش من إطلاق ذلك في غيره من الصفات.

[vii] الشهرستاني:

لعمري لقد طفت في تلك المعاهد كلها ... وسيرت طرفي بين تلك المعالم
فلم أر إلا واضعا كف حائر ... على ذقن أو قارعاً سن نادم

[viii]ابن تيمية في مجموع الفتاوى: وأما مخاطبة أهل اصطلاح باصطلاحهم ولغتهم فليس بمكروه، إذا احتيج إلى ذلك وكانت المعاني صحيحة، كمخاطبة العجم من الروم والفرس والترك بلغتهم وعرفهم، فإن هذا جائز حسن للحاجة. وإنما كرهه الأئمة إذا لم يحتج إليه. ولهذا قال النبي لأم خالد بنت خالد بن سعيد بن العاص – وكانت صغيرة ولدت بأرض الحبشة لأن أباها كان من المهاجرين إليها – فقال لها "يا أم خالد هذا سنا"، والسنا بلسان الحبشة الحسن، لأنها كانت من أهل هذه اللغة. وكذلك يترجم القرآن والحديث لمن يحتاج إلى تفهيمه إياه بالترجمة، وكذلك يقرأ المسلم ما يحتاج إليه من كتب الأمم وكلامهم بلغتهم، ويترجمها بالعربية. كما أمر النبي زيد بن ثابت أن يتعلم كتاب اليهود ليقرأ له ويكتب له ذلك حيث لم يأمن من اليهود عليه.

[ix]ابن تيمية في الدرء: ومما يوضح هذا أن العلم الإلهي لا يجوز أن يستدل فيه بقياس تمثيلي يستوي فيه الأصل والفرع، ولا بقياس شمولي تستوي فيه أفراده، فإن الله سبحانه ليس كمثله شيء، فلا يجوز أن يمثل بغيره، ولا يجوز أن يدخل تحت قضية كلية تستوي أفرادها. ولهذا لما سلك طوائف من المتفلسفة والمتكلمة مثل هذه الأقيسة في المطالب الإلهية، لم يصلوا بها إلى اليقين، بل تناقضت أدلتهم، وغلب عليهم بعد التناهي الحيرة والاضطراب، لما يرونه من فساد أدلتهم أو تكافئها. ولكن يستعمل في ذلك قياس الأولي، سواء كان تمثيلا أو شمولا، كما قال تعالي: {ولله المثل الأعلى} [النحل: 60] مثل أن يعلم أن كل كمال ثبت للممكن أو المحدث لا نقص فيه بوجه من الوجوه – وهو ما كان كمالا للموجود غير مستلزم للعدم – فالواجب القديم أولى به.

[x]ابن تيمية في الدرء: ولكن يستعمل في ذلك قياس الأولي، سواء كان تمثيلا أو

شمولا، كما قال تعالي: {ولله المثل الأعلى} [النحل: 60] ، مثل أن يعلم أن كل كمال ثبت للممكن أو المحدث لا نقص فيه بوجه من الوجوه - وهو ما كان كمالا للموجود غير مستلزم للعدم - فالواجب القديم أولى به.

[xi] قال عليه السلام: ما منكم من أحد إلا سيرى ربه مُخْلِيا به. فقال له أبو رَزِينٍ العُقَيلي (لقيط بن عامر المنتفق): كيف يا رسول الله وهو واحد ونحن جميع؟ فقال له النبي: سأنبئك مثل ذلك في آلاء الله؛ هذا القمر، كلكم يراه مُخْلِيا به، وهو آية من آيات الله، فالله تعالى أَكبر. [شعيب الأرناؤوط: إسناده ضعيف، والحديث حسن بشواهده] قال عليه السلام: ضحك ربنا من قنوط عباده وقرب غِيَرِه. [صححه السيوطي في الجامع الصغير] قال عليه السلام: ضحك ربنا عز وجل من قنوط عباده وقرب غِيَرِه، فقال أبو رزينٍ: أَوَيضحك الرب عز وجل؟ قال: نعم فقال: لن نعدم من رب يضحك خيرا. [حسنه الألباني بمجموع الطرق في الصحيحة، وضعفه شعيب الأرناؤوط في تخريج المسند.]

[xii] ابن تيمية في الدرء: وأما هذا القانون الذي وضعوه، فقد سبقهم إليه طائفة، منهم أبو حامد، وجعله قانونا في جواب المسائل التي سئل عنها في نصوص أشكلت على السائل، كالمسائل التي سأله عنها القاضي أبو بكر بن العربي، وخالفه القاضي أبو بكر العربي في كثير من تلك الأجوبة، وكان يقول: شيخنا أبو حامد دخل في بطون الفلاسفة ثم أراد أن يخرج منهم فما قدر.

[xiii] الغزالي في الإحياء: ومن ترقيهم إلى هذا الحد، زاد الفلاسفة فأولوا كل ما ورد في الآخرة وردوه إلى آلام عقلية وروحانية ولذات عقلية، وأنكروا حشر الأجساد، وقالوا ببقاء النفوس، وأنها تكون إما معذبة وإما منعمة بعذاب ونعيم لا يدرك بالحس. وهؤلاء هم المسرفون. وحد الاقتصاد بين هذا الانحلال كله وبين جمود الحنابلة دقيق غامض لا يطلع عليه إلا الموفقون الذين يدركون الأمور بنور إلهي، لا بالسماع، ثم إذا انكشفت لهم أسرار الأمور على ما هي عليه، نظروا إلى

السمع والألفاظ الواردة، فما وافق ما شاهدوه بنور اليقين قرروه وما خالف أولوه. فأما من يأخذ معرفة هذه الأمور من السمع المجرد فلا يستقر له فيها قدم ولا يتعين له موقف. والأليق بالمقتصر على السمع المجرد مقام أحمد بن حنبل رحمة الله.

[xiv]ابن رشد في فصل المقال: وأما الأشياء التي لخفائها لا تعلم إلا بالبرهان، فقد تلطف الله فيها لعباده الذين لا سبيل لهم إلى البرهان، إما من قبل فطرهم وإما من قبل عادتهم وإما من قبل عدمهم أسباب التعلم، بأن ضرب لهم أمثالها وأشباهها ودعاهم إلى التصديق بتلك الأمثال، إذ كانت تلك الأمثال يمكن أن يقع التصديق بها بالأدلة المشتركة للجميع، أعني الجدلية والخطابية. وهذا هو السبب في أن انقسم الشرع إلى ظاهر وباطن. فإن الظاهر هو تلك الأمثال المضروبة لتلك المعاني والباطن هو تلك المعاني التي لا تنجلي إلا لأهل البرهان.

[xv]التفتازاني في شرح المقاصد: فإن قيل: إذا كان الدين الحق نفي الحيز والجهة فما بال الكتب السماوية والأحاديث النبوية مشعرة في مواضع لا تحصى بثبوت ذلك، من غير أن يقع في موضع واحد تصريح بنفي ذلك؟ أجيب بأنه لما كان التنزيه عن الجهة مما تقصر عنه عقول العامة، حتى تكاد تجزم بنفي ما ليس في الجهة، كان الأنسب في خطاباتهم والأقرب إلى إصلاحهم والأليق بدعوتهم إلى الحق ما يكون ظاهراً في التشبيه.

[xvi]الرازي في أساس التقديس: اعلم أن الدلائل القطعية إذا قامت على ثبوت شيء، ثم وجدنا أدلة نقلية يشعر ظاهرها بخلاف ذلك، فهناك لا يخلو الحال من أحد أمور أربعة: إما أن يصدق مقتضى العقل والنقل، فيلزم تصديق النقيضين وهو محال، وإما أن يبطل، فيلزم تكذيب النقيضين وهو محال، وإما أن يصدق الظواهر النقلية، ويكذب الظواهر العقلية، وذلك باطل، لأنه لا يمكننا أن نعرف صحة الظواهر النقلية إلا إذا عرفنا بدلائل العقلية إثبات الصانع وصفاته وكيفية دلالة المعجزة على صدق الرسول - صلى الله عليه وسلم - وظهور المعجزات على محمد - صلى الله عليه

وسلم. ولو جوزنا القدح في الدلائل العقلية، صار العقل متهماً غير مقبول القول. ولو كان كذلك، لخرج أن يكون مقبول القول في هذه الأصول. وإذا لم تثبت هذه الأصول، خرجت الدلائل النقلية عن كونها مفيدة. فثبت أن القدح في العقل لتصحيح النقل يفضي إلى القدح في العقل والنقل معاً، وأنه باطل. ولما بطلت الأقسام الأربعة، لم يبق إلا أن يقطع بمقتضى الدلائل العقلية القاطعة بأن هذه الدلائل النقلية إما أن يقال إنها غير صحيحة، أو يقال إنها صحيحة، إلا أن المراد منها غير ظواهرها. ثم إن جوزنا التأويل، اشتغلنا به على سبيل التبرع بذكر تلك التأويلات على التفصيل. وإن لم يجز التأويل، فوضنا العلم بها إلى الله تعالى. فهذا هو القانون الكلي المرجوع إليه في جميع المتشابهات.

[xvii]ابن حجر في الفتح: واستدل أبو المظفر بن السمعاني بآيات الباب وأحاديثه على فساد طريقة المتكلمين في تقسيم الأشياء إلى جسم وجوهر وعرض. قالوا: فالجسم ما اجتمع من الافتراق، والجوهر ما حمل العرض، والعرض مالا يقوم بنفسه. وجعلوا الروح من الأعراض، وردوا الأخبار في خلق الروح قبل الجسد والعقل قبل الخلق، واعتمدوا على حدسهم وما يؤدي إليه نظرهم، ثم يعرضون عليه النصوص، فما وافقه قبلوه وما خالفه ردوه. ثم ساق هذه الآيات ونظائرها من الأمر بالتبليغ. قال: وكان مما أمر بتبليغه التوحيد، بل هو أصل ما أمر به، فلم يترك شيئا من أمور الدين أصوله وقواعده وشرائعه إلا بلغه، ثم لم يدع إلا الاستدلال بما تمسكوا به من الجوهر والعرض، ولا يوجد عنه ولا عن أحد من أصحابه من ذلك حرف واحد فما فوقه، فعرف بذلك أنهم ذهبوا خلاف مذهبهم وسلكوا غير سبيلهم بطريق محدث مخترع لم يكن عليه رسول الله – صلى الله عليه وسلم – ولا أصحابه رضي الله عنهم، ويلزم من سلوكه العود على السلف بالطعن والقدح ونسبتهم إلى قلة المعرفة واشتباه الطرق. فالحذر من الاشتغال بكلامهم والاكتراث بمقالاتهم، فإنها سريعة التهافت كثيرة التناقض. وما من كلام تسمعه لفرقة منهم إلا وتجد لخصومهم عليه كلاما يوازنه أو

يقاربه، فكل بكل مقابل، وبعض ببعض معارض. وحسبك من قبيح ما يلزم من طريقتهم أنا إذا جرينا على ما قالوه وألزمنا الناس بما ذكروه، لزم من ذلك تكفير العوام جميعا لأنهم لا يعرفون إلا الاتباع المجرد، ولو عرض عليهم هذا الطريق ما فهمه أكثرهم، فضلا عن أن يصير منهم صاحب نظر، وإنما غاية توحيدهم التزام ما وجدوا عليه أئمتهم في عقائد الدين والعض عليها بالنواجذ والمواظبة على وظائف العبادات وملازمة الأذكار بقلوب سليمة طاهرة عن الشبه والشكوك، فتراهم لا يحيدون عما اعتقدوه، ولو قطعوا إربا إربا، فهنيئا لهم هذا اليقين وطوبى لهم هذه السلامة. فإذا كفر هؤلاء، وهم السواد الأعظم وجمهور الأمة، فما هذا إلا طي بساط الإسلام وهدم منار الدين – والله المستعان.

[xviii]ابن عبد البر في التمهيد: أهل السنة مجموعون على الإقرار بالصفات الواردة كلها في القرآن والسنة والإيمان بها وحملها على الحقيقة لا على المجاز، إلا أنهم لا يكيفون شيئا من ذلك ولا يحدون فيه صفة محصورة. وأما أهل البدع والجهمية والمعتزلة كلها والخوارج، فكلهم ينكرها ولا يحمل شيئا منها على الحقيقة، ويزعمون أن من أقر بها مشبه، وهم عند من أثبتها نافون للمعبود. والحق فيما قاله القائلون بما نطق به كتاب الله وسنة رسوله وهم أئمة الجماعة – والحمد لله.

[xix]توضيح المقاصد شرح الكافية الشافية لابن القيم: نقول فيها ما قاله ربنا تبارك وتعالى وما قاله نبينا – صلى الله عليه وسلم. نصف الله تعالى بما وصف به نفسه وبما وصفه به رسوله، من غير تحريف ولا تعطيل ومن غير تشبيه ولا تمثيل، بل نثبت له سبحانه ما أثبته لنفسه من الأسماء والصفات وننفي عنه النقائص والعيوب ومشابهة المخلوقات، إثباتا بلا تمثيل وتنزيها بلا تعطيل. فمن شبه الله بخلقه فقد كفر، ومن جحد ما وصف الله به نفسه فقد كفر، وليس ما وصف الله به نفسه او وصفه به رسولا تشبيها. فالمشبه يعبد صنما والمعطل يعبد عدما والموحد يعبد إلها واحدا صمدا {ليس كمثله شيء وهو السميع البصير}.

[xx] التبصير في معالم الدين للطبري: فنثبت كل هذه المعاني التي ذكرنا أنها جاءت بها الأخبار والكتاب والتنزيل على ما يعقل من حقيقة الإثبات، وننفي عنه التشبيه؛ فنقول: يسمع - جل ثناؤه - الأصوات، لا بخرق في أذن، ولا جارحة كجوارح بني آدم. وكذلك يبصر الأشخاص ببصر لا يشبه أبصار بني آدم التي هي جوارح لهم. وله يدان ويمين وأصابع، وليست جارحة، ولكن يدان مبسوطتان بالنعم على الخلق، لا مقبوضتان عن الخير. ووجه لا كجوارح الخلق التي من لحم ودم. ونقول يضحك إلى من شاء من خلقه، ولا نقول إن ذلك كشر عن أسنان، ويهبط كل ليلة إلى السماء الدنيا.

[xxi]قول يحيى بن عمار في الحجة في بيان المحجة لقوام السنة الأصبهاني: لا نحتاج في هذا الباب إلى قول أكثر من هذا: أن نؤمن به، وننفي الكيفية عنه، ونتقي الشك فيه، ونوقن بأن ما قاله الله سبحانه وتعالى ورسوله - صلى الله عليه وسلم، ولا نتفكر في ذلك ولا نسلط عليه الوهم والخاطر والوسواس، وتعلم حقا يقينا أن كل ما تصور في همك ووهمك من كيفية أو تشبيه، فالله سبحانه بخلافه وغيره. نقول: هو بذاته على العرش، وعلمه محيط بكل شيء.

[xxii]ابن عبد البر في التمهيد: فإن قال إنه لا يكون مستويا على مكان إلا مقرونا بالتكييف، قيل قد يكون الاستواء واجبا والتكييف مرتفع، وليس رفع التكييف يوجب رفع الاستواء، ولو لزم هذا لزم التكييف في الأزل لأنه لا يكون كائن في لا مكان إلا مقرونا بالتكييف، وقد عقلنا وأدركنا بحواسنا أن لنا أرواحا في أبداننا ولا نعلم كيفية ذلك، وليس جهلنا بكيفية الأرواح يوجب أن ليس لنا أرواح، وكذلك ليس جهلنا بكيفية على عرشه يوجب أنه ليس على عرشه.

[xxiii]ابن تيمية في مجموع الفتاوى: لكن هذا النور والبركة والرحمة التي في القلوب هي من آثار ما وصف به نفسه من نزوله بذاته سبحانه وتعالى.

[xxiv]ابن عبد البر في التمهيد: وقال آخرون ينزل بذاته. أخبرنا أحمد بن عبد الله

أن أباه أخبره قال حدثنا أحمد بن خالد قال حدثنا يحيى بن عثمان بن صالح بمصر قال سمعت نعيم بن حماد يقول: حديث النزول يرد على الجهمية قولهم. قال: وقال نعيم ينزل بذاته، وهو على كرسيه. قال أبو عمر: ليس هذا بشيء عند أهل الفهم من أهل السنة، لأن هذا كيفية، وهم يفزعون منها لأنها لا تصلح إلا فيما يحاط به عيانا، وقد جل الله وتعالى عن ذلك. وما غاب عن العيون فلا يصفه ذوو العقول إلا بخبر، ولا خبر في صفات الله إلا ما وصف نفسه به في كتابه أو على لسان رسوله – صلى الله عليه وسلم، فلا نتعدى ذلك إلى تشبيه أو قياس أو تمثيل أو تنظير، فإنه ليس كمثله شيء وهو السميع البصير.

[xxv]الخطابي في معالم السنن: وقد زل بعض شيوخ أهل الحديث ممن يرجع إلى معرفته بالحديث والرجال، فحاد عن هذه الطريقة حين روى حديث النزول، ثم أقبل يسأل نفسه عليه، فقال إن قال قائل كيف ينزل ربنا إلى السماء؟ قيل له ينزل كيف شاء. فإن قال هل يتحرك إذا نزل أم لا؟ فقال إن شاء تحرك وإن شاء لم يتحرك. قلت: وهذا خطأ فاحش، والله سبحانه لا يوصف بالحركة، لأن الحركة والسكون يتعاقبان في محل واحد، وإنما يجوز أن يوصف بالحركة من يجوز أن يوصف بالسكون، وكلاهما من أعراض الحدث وأوصاف المخلوقين، والله جل وعز متعال عنهما، ليس كمثله شيء. فلو جرى هذا الشيخ – عفا الله عنا وعنه – على طريقة السلف الصالح، ولم يدخل نفسه فيما لا يعنيه، لم يكن يخرج به القول إلى مثل هذا الخطأ الفاحش.

[xxvi]ابن القيم في مختصر الصواعق: وأما الذين أمسكوا عن الأمرين وقالوا: لا نقول يتحرك وينتقل، ولا ننفي ذلك عنه، فهم أسعد بالصواب والاتباع، فإنهم نطقوا بما نطق به النص، وسكتوا عما سكت عنه، وتظهر صحة هذه الطريقة ظهورا تاما فيما إذا كانت الألفاظ التي سكت النص عنها مجملة محتملة لمعنيين: صحيح وفاسد، كلفظ الحركة والانتقال والجسم والحيز والجهة والأعراض والحوادث والعلة

والتغير والتركيب، ونحو ذلك من الألفاظ التي تحتها حق وباطل، فهذه لا تقبل مطلقا ولا ترد مطلقا، فإن الله سبحانه لم يثبت لنفسه هذه المسميات ولم ينفها عنه. فمن أثبتها مطلقا فقد أخطأ، ومن نفاها مطلقا فقد أخطأ، فإن معانيها منقسمة إلى ما يمتنع إثباته لله، وما يجب إثباته له، فإن الانتقال يراد به انتقال الجسم والعرض من مكان هو محتاج إليه إلى مكان آخر يحتاج إليه، وهو يمتنع إثباته للرب تعالى، وكذلك الحركة إذا أريد بها هذا المعنى امتنع إثباتها لله تعالى، ويراد بالحركة والانتقال حركة الفاعل من كونه فاعلا وانتقاله أيضا من كونه غير فاعل إلى كونه فاعلا.

[xxvii]ابن تيمية في الدرء: وأما الشرع فليس فيه ذكر هذه الأسماء في حق الله، لا بنفي ولا إثبات، ولم ينطق أحد من سلف الأمة وأئمتها في حق الله تعالى بذلك، لا نفيا ولا إثباتا، بل قول القائل: إن الله جسم أو ليس بجسم، أو جوهر أو ليس بجوهر، أو متحيز أو ليس بمتحيز، أو في جهة أو ليس في جهة، أو تقوم به الأعراض والحوادث أو لا تقوم به، ونحو ذلك ـــ،كل هذه الأقوال محدثة بين أهل الكلام المحدث، لم يتكلم السلف والأئمة فيها، لا بإطلاق النفي ولا بإطلاق الإثبات، بل كانوا ينكرون على أهل الكلام الذين يتكلمون بمثل هذا النوع في حق الله تعالي نفيا وإثباتا.

[xxviii]نقض الإمام أبي سعيد عثمان بن سعيد على المريسي الجهمي العنيد: وسئل ابن المبارك: بم نعرف ربنا؟ قال: "بأنه على العرش، بائن من خلقه." قيل: بحد؟ قال: "بحد." أخرجه عبد الله بن الإمام أحمد في السنة من طرق عن ابن شقي. وأخرجه الدارمي أيضا فِي الرد على الجهمية، والبيهقي فِي الأسماء والصفات من طريقين عن علي بن الحسن بن شقيق، عن ابن المبارك.

[xxix]نقض الإمام أبي سعيد عثمان بن سعيد على المريسي الجهمي العنيد: قال أبو سعيد: والله تعالى له حد لا يعلمه أحد غيره، ولا يجوز لأحد أن يتوهم لحده في نفسه، ولكن يؤمن بالحد ويكل علم ذلك إلى الله أيضا حد، وهو على عرشه فوق

سماواته، فهذان حدان اثنان.

[xxx] ابن تيمية في الدرء: فهذا ابن رشد يقول: والشبهة التي قادت نفاة الجهة إلى نفيها هو أنهم اعتقدوا أن إثبات الجهة يوجب إثبات المكان، وإثبات المكان يوجب إثبات الجسمية. قال: "ونحن نقول: إن هذا كله غير لازم، فإن الجهة غير المكان."

[xxxi] ابن عبد البر في التمهيد: وأما احتجاجهم أنه لو كان في مكان لأشبه المخلوقات، لأن ما أحاطت به الأمكنة واحتوته مخلوق، فشيء لا يلزم، ولا معنى له، لأنه عز وجل ليس كمثله شيء من خلقه، ولا يقاس بشيء من بريته، لا يدرك بقياس، ولا يقاس بالناس.

[xxxii] تفسير ابن كثير: وأما قوله تعالى ثم استوى على العرش، فللناس في هذا المقام مقالات كثيرة جدا ليس هذا موضع بسطها، وإنما نسلك في هذا المقام مذهب السلف الصالح مالك والأوزاعي والثوري والليث بن سعد والشافعي وأحمد وإسحاق بن راهويه وغيرهم من أئمة المسلمين قديما وحديثا، وهو إمرارها كما جاءت من غير تكييف ولا تشبيه ولا تعطيل. والظاهر المتبادر إلى أذهان المشبهين منفي عن الله، لا يشبهه شيء من خلقه، وليس كمثله شيء وهو السميع البصير، بل الأمر كما قال الأئمة، منهم نعيم بن حماد الخزاعي شيخ البخاري، قال: من شبه الله بخلقه كفر ومن جحد ما وصف الله به نفسه فقد كفر، وليس فيما وصف الله به نفسه ولا رسوله تشبيه. فمن أثبت لله تعالى ما وردت به الآيات الصريحة والأخبار الصحيحة على الوجه الذي يليق بجلال الله ونفى عن الله تعالى النقائص فقد سلك سبيل الهدى.

[xxxiii] ابن عبد البر في التمهيد: ولا ندفع ما وصف به نفسه لأنه دفع للقرآن. وقد قال الله عز وجل وجاء ربك والملك صفا صفا. وليس مجيئه حركة ولا زوالا ولا انتقالا، لأن ذلك إنما يكون إذا كان الجائي جسما أو جوهرا، فلما ثبت أنه ليس بجسم ولا جوهر، لم يجب أن يكون مجيئه حركة ولا نقلة. ولو اعتبرت ذلك

بقولهم جاءت فلانا قيامته، وجاءه الموت، وجاءه المرض، وشبه ذلك مما هو موجود نازل به، ولا مجيء، لبان لك - وبالله العصمة والتوفيق.

[xxxiv] الجواب الصحيح لمن بدل دين المسيح لابن تيمية: الوجه الثاني أن يقال: ما ذكرتموه عن المسلمين كذب ظاهر عليهم، فهذا النظم الذي ذكروه ليس هو في القرآن ولا في الحديث، ولا يعرف عالم مشهور من علماء المسلمين ولا طائفة مشهورة من طوائفهم، يطلقون العبارة التي حكوها عن المسلمين، حيث قالوا عنهم: "إنهم يقولون إن لله عينين يبصر بهما ويدين يبسطهما وساقا ووجها يوليه إلى كل مكان وجنباً." ولكن هؤلاء ركبوا من ألفاظ القرآن بسوء تصرفهم وفهمهم تركيبا زعموا أن المسلمين يطلقونه. والمقصود هنا أن الله - سبحانه وتعالى - إذا أضاف إلى نفسه ما أضافه إضافة يختص بها وتمنع أن يدخل فيها شيء من خصائص المخلوقين، وقد قال مع ذلك: إنه "ليس كمثله شيء" وإنه "لم يكن له كفوا أحد" وأنكر أن يكون له سمي، كان من فهم من هذه ما يختص به المخلوق، قد أتي من سوء فهمه ونقص عقله، لا من قصور في بيان الله ورسوله. ولا فرق في ذلك بين صفة وصفة، فمن فهم من علم الله ما يختص به المخلوق من أنه عرض محدث باضطرار أو اكتساب، فمن نفسه أتي، وليس في قولنا "علم الله" ما يدل على ذلك. كذلك من فهم من قوله "بل يداه مبسوطتان" الآية و "ما منعك أن تسجد لما خلقت بيدي" ما يختص به المخلوق من جوارحه وأعضائه، فمن نفسه أتي، فليس في ظاهر هذا اللفظ ما يدل على ما يختص به المخلوق كما في سائر الصفات. وكذلك إذا قال: "ثم استوى على العرش" فمن فهم من ذلك ما يختص بالمخلوق، كما يفهم من قوله :"فإذا استويت أنت ومن معك على الفلك" فمن نفسه أتي، فإن ظاهر اللفظ يدل على استواء يضاف إلى الله - عز وجل - كما يدل في تلك الآية على استواء يضاف إلى العبد. وإذا كان المستوي ليس مماثلا للمستوي، لم يكن الاستواء مماثلا للاستواء.

[xxxv]التبصير في معالم الدين للطبري: فإن يكن جائزاً أن يقال: سمع وأبصر من لا سمع له ولا بصر، إنه لجائز أن يقال: تكلم من لا كلام له، ورحم من لا رحمة له، وعاقب من لا عقاب له. وفي إحالة جميع الموافقين والمخالفين أن يقال: يتكلم من لا كلام له، أو يرحم من لا رحمة له، أو يعاقب من لا عقاب له، أدل دليل على خطأ قول القائل: يسمع من لا سمع له، ويبصر من لا بصر له. فنثبت كل هذه المعاني التي ذكرنا أنها جاءت بها الأخبار والكتاب والتنزيل على ما يعقل من حقيقة الإثبات، وننفي عنه التشبيه.

[xxxvi]ابن عبد البر في التمهيد: لأن علماء الصحابة والتابعين الذين حملت عنهم التأويل في القرآن قالوا في تأويل هذه الآية: "هو على العرش وعلمه في كل مكان،" وما خالفهم في ذلك أحد يحتج بقوله.

[xxxvii]ابن تيمية في الدرء: ومن الأخبار ما يكون ظاهره يبين المراد به لا يحتاج إلى دليل يصرفه عن ظاهره، ولكن يظن قوم أنه مما يفتقر إلى تأويل، كقوله: "الحجر السود يمين الله في الأرض، فمن صافحه وقبله فكأنما صافح الله وقبل يمينه." فهذا الخبر لو صح عن النبي - صلى الله عليه وسلم - لم يكن ظاهره أن الحجر صفة لله، بل صريح في أنه ليس صفة لله، لقوله "يمين الله في الأرض،" فقيده في الأرض، ولقوله "فمن صافحه فكأنما صافح الله،" والمشبه ليس هو المشبه به. وإذا كان صريحاً في أنه ليس صفة لله، لم يحتج إلى تأويل يخالف ظاهره.

[xxxviii]تفسير ابن رجب الحنبلي: وقال [أي ابن الجوزي]: كان أبو القاسم بن السمرقندي يقول إن أبا بكر بن الخاضبة كان يسمى ابن الفاعوس الحجري لأنه كان يقول الحجر الأسود يمين الله حقيقة. قلت [القائل ابن رجب]: إن صح عن ابن الفاعوس أنه كان يقول الحجر الأسود يمين الله حقيقة، فأصل ذلك أن طائفة من أصحابنا وغيرهم نفوا وقوع المجاز في القرآن، ولكن لا يعلم منهم من نفى المجاز في اللغة كقول أبي إسحاق الإسفرائيني. ولكن قد يسمع بعض صالحيهم إنكار

المجاز في القرآن، فيعتقد إنكاره مطلقا، ويؤيد ذلك أن المتبادر إلى فهم أكثر الناس من لفظ الحقيقة والمجاز المعاني والحقائق دون الألفاظ، فإذا قيل "إن هذا مجاز،" فهموا أنه ليس تحته معنى ولا له حقيقة، فينكرون ذلك وينفرون منه. ومن أنكر المجاز من العلماء، فقد ينكر إطلاق اسم المجاز لئلا يوهم هذا المعنى الفاسد ويصير ذريعة لمن يريد حقائق الكتاب والسنة ومدلولاتهما، ويقول غالب من تكلم بالحقيقة والمجاز هم المعتزلة ونحوهم من أهل البدع، وتطرقوا بذلك إلى تحريف الكلم عن مواضعه، فيمنع من التسمية بالمجاز، ويجعل جميع الألفاظ حقائق، ويقول: اللفظ إن دل بنفسه فهو حقيقة لذلك المعنى، وإن دل بقرينة فدلالته بالقرينة حقيقة للمعنى الآخر، فهو حقيقة في الحالين، وإن كان المعنى المدلول عليه مختلفا، فحينئذ يقال: لفظ اليمين في قوله سبحانه وتعالى: "والسماوات مطويات بيمينه" حقيقة، وهو دال على الصفة الذاتية، ولفظ اليمين في الحديث المعروف "الحجر الأسود يمين الله في الأرض، فمن صافحه فكأنما صافح الله عز وجل" وقيل: يمينه يراد به، مع هذه القرائن المحتفة به، محل الاستلام والتقبيل، وهو حقيقة في هذا المعنى في هذه الصورة، وليس فيه ما يوهم الصفة الذاتية أصلا، بل دلالته على معناه الخاص قطعية لا تحتمل النقيض بوجه، ولا تحتاج إلى تأويل ولا غيره. وإذا قيل: فابن الفاعوس لم يكن من أهل هذا الشأن - أعني البحث عن مدلولات الألفاظ، قيل: ولا ابن الخاضبة كان من أهله، وإن كان محدثا، وإنما سمع من ابن الفاعوس أو بلغه عنه إنكار أن يكون هذا مجازا، لما سمعه من إنكار لفظ المجاز، فحمله السامع لقصوره أو لهواه على أنه إذا كان حقيقة لزم أن يكون هو يد الرب عز وجل التي هي صفته، وهذا باطل، والله أعلم.

[xxxix] الذهبي في السير: ولكن الأولى في هذا ترك الخوض في حقيقة أو مجاز، فلا حاجة بنا إلى تقييد ما أطلقه السلف، بل نؤمن ونسكت، وقولنا في ذلك حقيقة أو مجازا ضرب من العي واللكن، فنزجر من بحث في ذلك - والله الموفق.

[xl] ابن تيمية في مجموع الفتاوى: وتمام الكلام في هذا الباب أنك تعلم أنا لا نعلم ما غاب عنا إلا بمعرفة ما شهدناه. فنحن نعرف أشياء بحسنا الظاهر أو الباطن، وتلك معرفة معينة مخصوصة، ثم إنا بعقولنا نعتبر الغائب بالشاهد، فيبقى في أذهاننا قضايا عامة كلية، ثم إذا خوطبنا بوصف ما غاب عنا لم نفهم ما قيل لنا إلا بمعرفة المشهود لنا. فلولا أنا نشهد من أنفسنا جوعا وعطشا وشبعا وريا وحبا وبغضا ولذة وألما ورضى وسخطا، لم نعرف حقيقة ما نخاطب به إذا وصف لنا ذلك وأخبرنا به عن غيرنا. وكذلك لو لم نعلم ما في الشاهد: حياة وقدرة وعلما وكلاما، لم نفهم ما نخاطب به إذا وصف الغائب عنا بذلك. وكذلك لو لم نشهد موجودا، لم نعرف وجود الغائب عنا. فلا بد فيما شهدناه وما غاب عنا من قدر مشترك هو مسمى اللفظ المتواطئ. فبهذه الموافقة والمشاركة والمشابهة والمواطأة، نفهم الغائب ونثبته، وهذا خاصة العقل. ولولا ذلك، لم نعلم إلا ما نحسه ولم نعلم أمورا عامة ولا أمورا غائبة عن إحساسنا الظاهرة والباطنة. ولهذا من لم يحس الشيء ولا نظيره، لم يعرف حقيقته. ثم إن الله تعالى أخبرنا بما وعدنا به في الدار الآخرة من النعيم والعذاب، وأخبرنا بما يؤكل ويشرب وينكح ويفرش وغير ذلك. فلولا معرفتنا بما يشبه ذلك في الدنيا، لم نفهم ما وعدنا به. ونحن نعلم مع ذلك أن تلك الحقائق ليست مثل هذه، حتى قال ابن عباس – رضي الله عنه – ليس في الدنيا مما في الجنة إلا الأسماء، وهذا تفسير قوله "وأتوا به متشابها" على أحد الأقوال. فبين هذه الموجودات في الدنيا وتلك الموجودات في الآخرة مشابهة وموافقة واشتراك من بعض الوجوه، وبه فهمنا المراد وأحببناه ورغبنا فيه أو أبغضناه ونفرنا عنه، وبينهما مباينة ومفاضلة لا يقدر قدرها في الدنيا. وهذا من التأويل الذي لا نعلمه نحن بل يعلمه الله تعالى.

ابن تيمية في الدرء: ما من موجودين إلا بينهما قدر مشترك وقدر مميز، فإنهما لا بد أن يشتركا في أنهما موجودان ثابتان حاصلان، وأنّ كلا منهما له حقيقة هي ذاته ونفسه وماهيته، حتى لو كان الموجودان مختلفين اختلافا ظاهرا كالسواد والبياض،

فلا بد أن يشتركا في مسمى الوجود والحقيقة ونحو ذلك، بل وفيما هو أخص من ذلك مثل كون كل منهما لونا وعرضا وقائما بغيره ونحو ذلك، وهما مع هذا مختلفان.

ابن تيمية في مجموع الفتاوى: ومن الناس من يسمي هذه الأسماء المشكّكة لكون المعنى في أحد المحلين أكمل منه في الآخر، فإن الوجود بالواجب أحق منه بالممكن، والبياض بالثلج أحق منه بالعاج، وأسماؤه وصفاته من هذا الباب، فإن الله تعالى يوصف بها على وجه لا يماثل أحدا من المخلوقين، وإن كان بين كل قسمين قدرا مشتركا، وذلك القدر المشترك هو مسمى اللفظ عند الإطلاق، فإذا قيّد بأحد المحلين تقيد به ... ومعلوم بالضرورة من دين المسلمين أن الله مستحق للأسماء الحسنى، وقد سمى بعض عباده ببعض تلك الأسماء كما سمى العبد سميعا بصيرا وحيّا وعليما وحكيما ورؤوفا رحيما وملكا وعزيزا ومؤمنا وكريما وغير ذلك، مع العلم بأن الاتفاق في الاسم لا يوجب مماثلة الخالق بالمخلوق، وإنما يوجب الدلالة على أن بين المسميين قدرا مشتركا فقط، مع أن المميز الفارق أعظم من المشترك الجامع ... وقد تدبرت كلام عامة من ينفي شيئا مما أثبته الرسل من الأسماء والصفات فوجدتهم كلهم متناقضين، فإنهم يحتجون لما نفوه بنظير ما يحتج به النافي لما أثبتوه، فيلزمهم إما إثبات الأمرين وإما نفيهما، فإذا نفوهما فلا بد لهم أن يقولوا بالواجب الوجود وعدمه جميعا، وهذا نهاية هؤلاء النفاة الملاحدة الغلاة من القرامطة وغلاة المتفلسفة، فإنهم إذا أخذوا ينفون النقيضين جميعا، فالنقيضان كما أنهما لا يجتمعان، فلا يرتفعان.

[xli] ابن عبد البر في التمهيد: ومن حق الكلام أن يحمل على حقيقته حتى تتفق الأمة أنه أريد به المجاز، إذ لا سبيل إلى اتباع ما أنزل إلينا من ربنا إلا على ذلك، وإنما يوجه كلام الله – عز وجل – إلى الأشهر والأظهر من وجوهه ما لم يمنع من ذلك ما يجب له التسليم. ولو ساغ ادعاء المجاز لكل مدع، ما ثبت شيء من

العبارات وجل الله – عز وجل – عن أن يخاطب إلا بما تفهمه العرب في معهود مخاطباتها.

[xlii]التفتازاني في شرح المقاصد: فإن قيل: إذا كان الدين الحق نفي الحيز والجهة فما بال الكتب السماوية والأحاديث النبوية مشعرة في مواضع لا تحصى بثبوت ذلك، من غير أن يقع في موضع واحد تصريح بنفي ذلك؟ أجيب بأنه لما كان التنزيه عن الجهة مما تقصر عنه عقول العامة، حتى تكاد تجزم بنفي ما ليس في الجهة، كان الأنسب في خطاباتهم والأقرب إلى إصلاحهم والأليق بدعوتهم إلى الحق ما يكون ظاهراً في التشبيه.

[xliii]سنن الترمذي: وقد قال غير واحد من أهل العلم في هذا الحديث وما يشبه هذا من الروايات من الصفات ونزول الرب تبارك وتعالى كل ليلة إلى السماء الدنيا، قالوا: قد تثبت الروايات في هذا ويؤمن بها ولا يتوهم ولا يقال كيف. هكذا روي عن مالك، وسفيان بن عيينة، وعبد الله بن المبارك، أنهم قالوا في هذه الأحاديث: "أمروها بلا كيف،" وهكذا قول أهل العلم من أهل السنة والجماعة. وأما الجهمية، فأنكرت هذه الروايات وقالوا: هذا تشبيه، وقد ذكر الله عز وجل في غير موضع من كتابه اليد والسمع والبصر، فتأولت الجهمية هذه الآيات ففسروها على غير ما فسر أهل العلم، وقالوا: إن الله لم يخلق آدم بيده، وقالوا: إن معنى اليد هاهنا القوة،" وقال إسحاق بن إبراهيم: "إنما يكون التشبيه إذا قال يد كيد، أو مثل يد، أو سمع كسمع، أو مثل سمع، فإذا قال: سمع كسمع، أو مثل سمع، فهذا التشبيه، وأما إذا قال كما قال الله تعالى يد وسمع وبصر، ولا يقول كيف، ولا يقول مثل سمع ولا كسمع، فهذا لا يكون تشبيها، وهو كما قال الله تعالى في كتابه: "ليس كمثله شيء وهو السميع البصير."

[xliv]الفقه الأكبر لأبي حنيفة: وله يد ووجه ونفس كما ذكره الله تعالى في القرآن. فما ذكره الله تعالى في القرآن من ذكر الوجه واليد والنفس، فهو له صفات

بلا كيف، ولا يقال إن يده قدرته أو نعمته، لأن فيه إبطال الصفة، وهو قول أهل القدر والاعتزال. ولكن يده صفته بلا كيف وغضبه ورضاه صفتان من صفات الله تعالى بلا كيف.

[xlv] أبو الحسن في المقالات: قال أهل السنة وأصحاب الحديث ليس بجسم ولا يشبه الأشياء، وأنه استوى على العرش كما قال "الرحمن على العرش استوى" [طه] ولا يتقدم بين يدي الله في القول، بل نقول استوى بلا كيف.

[xlvi]الجويني في الإرشاد عن ذم التفويض: الإعراض عن التأويل حذرا من مواقعة محذور في الاعتقاد يجر إلى اللبس والإبهام، واستزلال العوام، وتطرق الشبهات إلى أصول الدين، وتعريض لبعض من كتاب الله لرجم الظنون.

[xlvii]الجويني في النظامية عن ذم التأويل: اختلف مسالك العلماء في الظواهر التي وردت في الكتاب والسنة، وامتنع على أهل الحق فحواها وإجراؤها على موجب ما تبرزه أفهام أرباب اللسان منها. فرأى بعضهم تأويلها، والتزام هذا المنهج في آي الكتاب، وفيما صح من سنن النبي - صلى الله عليه وسلم. وذهب أئمة السلف إلى الانكفاف عن التأويل، وإجراء الظواهر على مواردها، وتفويض معانيها إلى الرب سبحانه. والذي نرتضيه رأيا وندين الله به عقدا اتباع سلف الأمة؛ فالأولى الاتباع وترك الابتداع، والدليل السمعي القاطع في ذلك أن إجماع الأمة حجة متبعة، وهو مستند معظم الشريعة، وقد درج صحب الرسول - صلى الله عليه وسلم - على ترك التعرض لمعانيها ودرك ما فيها، وهم صفوةُ الإسلام والمشتغلون بأعباء الشريعة، وكانوا لا يألون جهدا في ضبط قواعد الملة، والتواصي بحفظها، وتعليم الناس ما يحتاجون إليه منها. فلو كان تأويل هذه الظواهر مسوغا أو محتوما، لأوشك أن يكون اهتمامهم بها فوق اهتمامهم بفروع الشريعة، فإذا انصرم عصرهم وعصر التابعين على الإضراب عن التأويل، كان ذلك قاطعا بأنه الوجه المتبع بحق. فعلى ذي الدين أن يعتقد تنزه الرب تعالى عن صفات المحدثات، ولا يخوض في تأويل المشكلات،

ويكل معناها إلى الرب. ومما استحسن من إمام دار الهجرة مالك بن أنس، أنه سئل عن قوله تعالى: "الرَّحْمَنُ عَلَى الْعَرْشِ اسْتَوَى" [طه: 5]، فقال: الاستواء معلوم، والكيف مجهول، والسؤال عنه بدعة. فلتجر آية الاستواء والمجيء وقوله: "لِمَا خَلَقْتُ بِيَدَيَّ"، "وَيَبْقَى وَجْهُ رَبِّكَ" [الرحمن: 27]، وقوله: "تَجْرِي بِأَعْيُنِنَا" [القمر: 4]، وما صح عن الرسول عليه السلام - كخبر النزول وغيره - على ما ذكرنا؛ فهذا بيان ما يجب لله تعالى.

[xlviii]الباقلاني في تمهيد الأوائل وتلخيص الدلائل: فإن قالوا: فما أنكرتم أن يكون المعنى في قوله "خلقت بيدي" أنه خلقه بقدرته أو بنعمته، لأن اليد في اللغة قد تكون بمعنى النعمة وبمعنى القدرة، كما يقال لي عند فلان يد بيضاء، يراد به نعمة، وكما يقال هذا الشيء في يد فلان وتحت يد فلان، يراد به أنه تحت قدرته وفي ملكه، ويقال رجل أيد إذا كان قادرا ... فكذلك قوله "خلقت بيدي" يعني بقدرتي أو نعمتي، يقال لهم: هذا باطل، لأن قوله "بيدي" يقتضي إثبات يدين هما صفة له، فلو كان المراد بهما القدرة، لوجب أن يكون له قدرتان، وأنتم فلا تزعمون أن للباري سبحانه قدرة واحدة، فكيف يجوز أن تثبتوا له قدرتين. وقد أجمع المسلمون من مثبتي الصفات والنافين لها على أنه لا يجوز أن يكون له تعالى قدرتان، فبطل ما قلتم. وكذلك لا يجوز أن يكون الله تعالى خلق آدم بنعمتين، لأن نعم الله تعالى على آدم وعلى غيره لا تحصى ... ويدل على فساد تأويلهم أيضا أنه لو كان الأمر على ما قالوه، لم يغفل عن ذلك إبليس، وعن أن يقول: وأي فضل لآدم علي يقتضي أن أسجد له، وأنا أيضا بيدك خلقتني، التي هي قدرتك، وبنعمتك خلقتني. وفي العلم بأنه الله تعالى فضل آدم عليه بخلقه بيديه دليل على فساد ما قالوه، فإن قال قائل: فما أنكرتم أن يكون وجهه ويده جارحة، إذ كنتم لم تعقلوا يد صفة ووجه صفة لا جارحة، يقال له: لا يجب ذلك، كما لا يجب إذا لم نعقل حيا عالما قادرا إلا جسما أن نقضي نحن وأنتم على الله تعالى بذلك، وكما لا يجب متى كان قائما بذاته أن يكون

جوهرا أو جسما، لأنا وإياكم لم نجد قائما بنفسه في شاهدنا إلا كذلك.

[xlix] الجويني في الإرشاد عن الصفات الخبرية (اليدان والعينان والوجه): ومن سلك من أصحابنا سبيل إثبات هذه الصفات بظواهر هذه الآيات ألزمه سوق كلامه أن يجعل الاستواء والمجيء والنزول والجنب من الصفات تمسكا بالظاهر، فإن ساغ تأويلها فيما يتفق عليه، لم يبعد أيضا طريق التأويل فيما ذكرناه.

[l] ابن عربي في الفتوحات المكية: وقسم آخر قال: نؤمن بهذا اللفظ كما جاء من غير أن نعقل له معنى حتى نكون في هذا الإيمان به في حكم من لم يسمع، ونبقى على ما أعطانا دليل العقل من إحالة مفهوم هذا الظاهر من هذا القول. فهذا القسم متحكم أيضا بحسن عبارة، وأنه رد على الله بحسن عبارة، فإنهم جعلوا نفوسهم في حكم نفوس لم تسمع ذلك الخطاب. وقسم آخر قالوا: نؤمن بهذا اللفظ على حد علم الله فيه، وعلم رسوله - صلى الله عليه وسلم. فهؤلاء قد قالوا: إن الله خاطبنا عبثاً، لأنه خاطبنا بما لا نفهم، والله يقول: "وَمَا أَرْسَلْنَا مِن رَّسُولٍ إِلاَّ بِلِسَانِ قَوْمِهِ لِيُبَيِّنَ لَهُمْ" [إبراهيم:4]. وقد جاء بهذا، فقد أبان كما قال الله، لكن أبى هؤلاء أن يكون ذلك بيانا.

[li] السنن الكبرى للبيهقي: ثنا الوليد بن مسلم قال: سئل الأوزاعي ومالك وسفيان الثوري والليث بن سعد عن هذه الأحاديث التي جاءت في التشبيه، فقالوا: أمروها كما جاءت بلا كيفية.

[lii] ابن تيمية في مجموع الفتاوى: فلو كانت دلالتها منتفية لكان الواجب أن يقال: أمروا لفظها مع اعتقاد أن المفهوم منها غير مراد؛ أو أمروا لفظها مع اعتقاد أن الله لا يوصف بما دلت عليه حقيقة وحينئذ فلا تكون قد أمرت كما جاءت ولا يقال حينئذ بلا كيف، إذ نفي الكيف عما ليس بثابت لغو من القول.

[liii] صحيح البخاري معلقا وقد غلق - قال أبو العالية: {استوى إلى السماء} [البقرة: 29]: «ارتفع»، {فسواهن} [البقرة: 29]: «خلقهن» وقال مجاهد:

{استوى} [البقرة: 29]: «علا» {على العرش}.

[liv] الغزالي في الإحياء: ومن ترقيهم إلى هذا الحد، زاد الفلاسفة فأولوا كل ما ورد في الآخرة وردوه إلى آلام عقلية وروحانية ولذات عقلية، وأنكروا حشر الأجساد، وقالوا ببقاء النفوس، وأنها تكون إما معذبة وإما منعمة بعذاب ونعيم لا يدرك بالحس. وهؤلاء هم المسرفون. وحد الاقتصاد بين هذا الانحلال كله وبين جمود الحنابلة دقيق غامض لا يطلع عليه إلا الموفقون الذين يدركون الأمور بنور إلهي، لا بالسماع، ثم إذا انكشفت لهم أسرار الأمور على ما هي عليه، نظروا إلى السمع والألفاظ الواردة، فما وافق ما شاهدوه بنور اليقين قرروه وما خالف أولوه. فأما من يأخذ معرفة هذه الأمور من السمع المجرد فلا يستقر له فيها قدم ولا يتعين له موقف. والأليق بالمقتصر على السمع المجرد مقام أحمد بن حنبل رحمة الله.

[lv]ابن القيم في مدارج السالكين: فاعلم أن مراد الشيخ وأمثاله من العارفين أهل الاستقامة ألا يقصر نظر القلب على صفة من الصفات، بحيث يستغرق فيها وحدها، بل يكون التفاته وشهوده واقعا على الذات الموصوفة بصفات الكمال المنعوتة بنعوت الجلال، فحينئذ يكون شهوده واقعا على الذات والصفات جميعا. ولا ريب أن هذا فوق مشهد الصفة الواحدة أو الصفات. ولكن يقال: الشهود لا يقع على الصفة المجردة، ولا يصح تجردها في الخارج ولا في الذهن، بل متى شهد الصفة شهد قيامها بالموصوف ولا بد، فما هذا الشهود الذاتي الذي هو فوق الشهود الوصفي؟ والأمر يرجع إلى شيء واحد، وهو أن من كان بصفات الله أعرف ولها أثبت، ومعارض الإثبات منتف عنده كان أكمل شهودا، ولهذا كان أكمل الخلق شهودا من قال: لا أحصي ثناء عليك، أنت كما أثنيت على نفسك. ولكمال معرفته بالأسماء والصفات، استدل بما عرفه منها على أن الأمر فوق ما أحصاه وعلمه. فمشهد الصفات مشهد الرسل والأنبياء وورثتهم، وكل من كان بها أعرف كان بالله أعلم، وكان مشهده بحسب ما عرف منها. وليس للعبد في الحقيقة مشاهدة ولا مكاشفة،

لا للذات ولا للصفات، أعني مشاهدة عيان وكشف عيان، وإنما هو مزيد إيمان وإيقان.

[lvi]ابن القيم في مدارج السالكين: الفرق الثاني أن الصفات الذاتية لا يطلق عليها اسم النعوت، كالوجه واليدين والقدم والأصابع' وتسمى صفات، وقد أطلق عليها السلف هذا الاسم، وكذلك متكلمو أهل الإثبات سموها صفات، وأنكر بعضهم هذه التسمية، كأبي الوفاء بن عقيل وغيره، وقال: لا ينبغي أن يقال: نصوص الصفات، بل آيات الإضافات؛ لأن الحي لا يوصف بيده ولا وجهه، فإن ذلك هو الموصوف، فكيف تسمى صفة؟ وأيضا: فالصفة معنى يعم الموصوف، فلا يكون الوجه واليد صفة. والتحقيق أن هذا نزاع لفظي في التسمية، فالمقصود إطلاق هذه الإضافات عليه سبحانه ونسبتها إليه والإخبار عنه بها، منزهة عن التمثيل والتعطيل، سواء سميت صفات أو لم تسم.

[lvii] ابن تيمية في الدرء: وكان الناس قبل أبي محمد بن كلاب صنفين، فأهل السنة والجماعة يثبتون ما يقوم بالله تعالى من الصفات والأفعال التي يشاؤها ويقدر عليها، والجهمية من المعتزلة وغيرهم تنكر هذا وهذا، فأثبت ابن كلاب قيام الصفات اللازمة به، ونفى أن يقوم به ما يتعلق بمشيئته وقدرته من الأفعال وغيرها، ووافقه على ذلك أبو العباس القلانسي وأبو الحسن الأشعري وغيرهما، وأما الحارث المحاسبي فكان ينتسب إلى قول ابن كلاب، ولهذا أمر أحمد بهجره، وكان أحمد يحذر من ابن كلاب وأتباعه، ثم قيل عن الحارث إنه رجع عن قوله.

[lviii]ابن تيمية في الدرء: ويراد بالمركب في عرفهم الخاص ما تميز منه شيء، كتميز العلم عن القدرة، وتميز ما يرى ونحو ذلك. وتسمية هذا المعنى تركيبا وضع وضعوه ليس موافقا للغة العرب، ولا لغة أحد من الأمم. وإن كان هذا مركبا، فكل ما في الوجود مركب، فإنه ما من موجود إلا ولا بد أن يعلم منه شيء دون شيء، والمعلوم ليس الذي هو غير معلوم. وقولهم إنه مفتقر إلى جزئه تلبيس، فإن الموصوف

بالصفات اللازمة له يمتنع أن تفارقه أو يفارقها، وليست له حقيقة غير الذات الموصوفة حتى يقال إن تلك الحقيقة مفتقرة إلى غيرها. والصفة اللازمة يسميها بعض الناس غير الموصوف، وبعض الناس يقول ليست غير الموصوف.

[lix] تفسير القرطبي: هذه مسألة الاستواء، وللعلماء فيها كلام وإجراء. وقد بينا أقوال العلماء فيها في "الكتاب الأسنى في شرح أسماء الله الحسنى وصفاته العلى" وذكرنا فيها هناك أربعة عشر قولا. والأكثر من المتقدمين والمتأخرين أنه إذا وجب تنزيه الباري سبحانه عن الجهة والتحيز، فمن ضرورة ذلك ولواحقه اللازمة عليه عند عامة العلماء المتقدمين وقادتهم من المتأخرين تنزيهه تبارك وتعالى عن الجهة، فليس بجهة فوق عندهم، لأنه يلزم من ذلك عندهم متى اختص بجهة أن يكون في مكان أو حيز، ويلزم على المكان والحيز الحركة والسكون للمتحيز والتغير والحدوث. هذا قول المتكلمين. وقد كان السلف الأول - رضي الله عنهم - لا يقولون بنفي الجهة ولا ينطقون بذلك، بل نطقوا هم والكافة بإثباتها لله تعالى كما نطق كتابه وأخبرت رسله، ولم ينكر أحد من السلف الصالح أنه استوى على عرشه حقيقة. وخص العرش بذلك لأنه أعظم مخلوقاته، وإنما جهلوا كيفية الاستواء، فإنه لا تعلم حقيقته. قال مالك رحمه الله: الاستواء معلوم - يعني في اللغة - والكيف مجهول، والسؤال عن هذا بدعة. وكذا قالت أم سلمة رضي الله عنها.

[lx] ابن تيمية في مجموع الفتاوى: والمخلوق، وإن كان صمداً من بعض الوجوه، فإن حقيقة الصمدية منتفية عنه، فإنه يقبل التفرق والتجزئة، وهو أيضاً محتاج إلى غيره، فإن كل ما سوى الله محتاج إليه من كل وجه، فليس أحد يصمد إليه كل شيء ولا يصمد إلى شيء إلا الله تبارك وتعالى.

[lxi] ابن تيمية في بيان تلبيس الجهمية: ولا ريب أن الرازي ونحوه ممن يحتج بمثل هذه الحجة لا يفسرون الانقسام هنا بهذا الذي قررناه من فصل بعضه عن بعض بحيث يكون كل بعض في حيزين منفصلين أو إمكان ذلك فيه، فإن أحداً لم يقل إن

الله منقسم بهذا الاعتبار.

[lxii] ابن تيمية في الجواب الصحيح: فمن هؤلاء من أطلق عليه لفظ "الجسم،" وأراد به القائم بنفسه أو الموجود، كما أطلق هؤلاء لفظ الجوهر، وقالوا: أردنا بالجوهر القائم بنفسه، وكما قال هؤلاء ليس في الوجود إلا جوهر أو عرض، فإن الوجود إما قائم بنفسه، وهو الجوهر، أو بغيره، وهو العرض، والجوهر أشرف القسمين.

[lxiii]أبو الحسن في الإبانة: قيل لهم: ولم قضيتم أن اليد إذا لم تكن نعمة لم تكن إلا جارحة؟ وإن رجعونا إلى شاهدنا، أو إلى ما نجده فيما بيننا من الخلق فقالوا: اليد إذا لم تكن نعمة في الشاهد لم تكن إلا جارحة. قيل لهم: إن عملتم على الشاهد وقضيتم به على الله تعالى، فكذلك لم نجد حيا من الخلق إلا جسما لحما ودما، فاقضوا بذلك على الله - تعالى عن ذلك - وإلا كنتم لقولكم تاركين ولاعتلالكم ناقضين. وإن أثبتم حيا لا كالأحياء منا، فلم أنكرتم أن تكون اليدان اللتان أخبر الله تعالى عنهما يدين ليستا نعمتين ولا جارحتين، ولا كالأيدي؟

[lxiv]ابن تيمية في مجموع الفتاوى: والجمع بين علوه وقربه ودنوه ونزوله سهل باعتبار شأن الروح في عملها وأحكامها، وهي مخلوقة، فكيف بالخالق سبحانه. إن روح الإنسان لا تزال في بدنه لا تخرج إلا بالموت، ومع ذلك في النوم قد تعرج إلى السماوات، وقد تبلغ العرش، وقد يؤذن لها في السجود (ما لم يكن جنبا)، ثم تعود إلى البدن، وذلك ثابت بالكتاب والسنة، بل وفي حال اليقظة، تعرج روح الداعي والساجد فتقرب من الله، فيسيرٌ على الله الخالق أن يكون فوق عرشه، ويقرب من عبده حيث يشاء. فعلى هذا، إن كانت الروح مما يشار إليها ويتبعها بصر الميت، كما قال - صلى الله عليه وسلم: "إن الروح إذا خرجت تبعها البصر وأنها تقبض ويعرج بها إلى السماء،" كانت الروح جسماً بهذا الاصطلاح. والمقصود أن الروح إذا كانت موجودة حية عالمة قادرة سميعة بصيرة، تصعد وتنزل وتذهب وتجيء

ونحو ذلك من الصفات، والعقول قاصرة عن تكييفها وتحديدها، لأنهم لم يشاهدوا لها نظيراً.، والشيء إنما تدرك حقيقته بمشاهدته أو مشاهدة نظيره، فإذا كانت الروح متصفة بهذه الصفات، مع عدم مماثلتها لما يشاهد من المخلوقات، فالخالق أولى بمباينته لمخلوقاته، مع اتصافه بما يستحقه من أسمائه وصفاته. وأهل العقول هم أعجز عن أن يحدوه أو يكيفوه منهم عن أن يحدوا الروح أو يكيفوها. فإذا كان من نفى صفات الروح جاحدا معطلا لها، ومن مثلها بما يشاهده من المخلوقات جاهلا ممثلا لها بغير شكلها، وهي مع ذلك ثابتة بحقيقة الإثبات، مستحقة لما لها من الصفات، فالخالق - سبحانه وتعالى - أولى أن يكون من نفى صفاته جاحدا معطلا، ومن قاسه بخلقه جاهلا به ممثلا، وهو سبحانه وتعالى ثابت بحقيقة الإثبات، مستحق لما له من الأسماء والصفات.

[lxv] ابن تيمية في الدرء: فإذا قال: أنا أصفه لا بهذا ولا بهذا، بل أنفي عنه هذين الوصفين المتقابلين، لأن اتصافه بأحدهما إنما يكون لو كان قابلا لأحدهما، وهو لا يقبل واحدا منهما، لأنه لو قبل ذلك لكان جسما، إذ هذه من صفات الأجسام، فإذا قدرنا موجودا ليس بجسم، لم يقبل لا هذا ولا هذا، قيل له: فهكذا سائر الملاحدة، إذا قالوا: لا نصفه لا بالحياة ولا بالموت، ولا العلم ولا الجهل، ولا القدرة ولا العجز.

[lxvi] الغزالي في تهافت الفلاسفة: قلنا: قول القائل كل تركيب يحتاج إلى مركب كقوله كل موجود يحتاج إلى موجد، فيقال له: الأول موجود قديم لا علة له ولا موجد. فكذلك يقال: هو موصوف قديم، ولا علة لذاته ولا لصفته ولا لقيام صفته بذاته، بل الكل قديم بلا علة. وأما الجسم، فإنما لم يجز أن يكون هو الأول لأنه حادث من حيث أنه لا يخلو عن الحوادث، ومن لم يثبت له حدوث الجسم، يلزمه أن يجوز أن تكون العلة الأولى جسما كما سنلزمه عليكم من بعد.

ابن تيمية في الدرء: وذلك أن هؤلاء قالوا لأبي حامد والمثبتين: إذا أثبتم ذاتاً

وصفة وحلولاً للصفة بالذات، فهو مركب، وكل مركب يحتاج إلى مركب. قال لهم: قول القائل كل مركب يحتاج إلى مركب كقول القائل كل موجود يحتاج إلى موجد. ومقصوده بذلك أن هذا المعنى الذي سميتموه تركيباً ليس معنى كونه مركباً إلا كون الذات موصوفة بصفات قائمة بها، ليس معناه أنه كان هناك شيء متفرق فركبه مركب، بل ولا هناك شيء يقبل التفريق، فإن الكلام إنما هو في إثبات صفات واجب الوجود اللازمة. فأبو حامد وأمثاله خاطبوا هؤلاء بلغتهم في أن الموصوف بصفة لازمة له يسمى مركبا وقالوا لهم قلتم إن مثل هذا المعنى الذي سميتموه تركيبا يمتنع في الواجب الوجود، فقولهم إن كل مركب مفتقر إلى مركب مغلطة نشأت من الإجمال في لفظ مركب، فإنهم لم يسلموا لهم أن هناك تركيبا هو فعل مركب حتى يقال إن المركب يفتقر إلى مركب، بل هناك ذات موصوفة بصفات لازمة. له فإذا قال القائل: كل موصوف بصفات لازمة له يفتقر إلى مركب ومؤلف يجمع بين الذات والصفات، كان قوله باطلا، فقولهم في هذا الموضع كل مركب يفتقر إلى مركب من هذا الباب.

[lxvii] ابن تيمية في مجموع الفتاوى: وذلك أنه قد علم بضرورة العقل أنه لا بد من موجود قديم غني عما سواه، إذ نحن نشاهد حدوث المحدثات كالحيوان والمعدن والنبات، والحادث ممكن ليس بواجب ولا ممتنع. وقد علم بالاضطرار أن المحدث لا بد له من محدث والممكن لا بد له من موجد، كما قال تعالى: "أم خلقوا من غير شيء أم هم الخالقون". فإذا لم يكونوا خلقوا من غير خالق، ولا هم الخالقون لأنفسهم، تعين أن لهم خالقا خلقهم.

Printed in Great Britain
by Amazon

42389425R00108